20 SONGS DONIZETTI

John Glenn Paton, Editor

Front cover art: *Napoli vista da Capodimonte, 1813, by Alexandre Hyacinthe Dunouy (French 1757–1843).*
Oil on canvas, 129 x 180.5 cm. Museo Nazionale di Capodimonte, Naples, Italy.

This exquisite landscape is a view of Naples as seen from the Royal Palace of Capodimonte, which is now an art museum.
The artist is looking southeast across the famous Bay of Naples toward the active volcano Vesuvius, beyond which lie the
ruins of Pompeii. Today, Capodimonte is the site of a world-renowned porcelain factory.

Back cover art: *Portrait of Donizetti by Domenico Induno (Italian 1815–1878),*
Museo Civico Bibliografico Musicale di Bologna, Italy.

This striking portrait displays a Romantic sensibility and sensitivity to its subject that is unique
among paintings of Donizetti.

Cover and interior design: Sue Hartman
Interior production: Linda Lusk and Greg Plumblee

Art direction: Holly DeBord
Project manager: Mary Kate Karr

*Gaetano Donizetti. This formal portrait was drawn by J. Kriehuber
in Vienna in 1842. The original drawing was converted into a widely
circulated lithograph. This image is taken from the cover of* Giovanna Grey,
published after Donizetti's death, by Francesco Lucca, Milan.

Table of Contents

Preface

"Do you want an autobiography? Here it is:
Born Bergamo at the end of November (1797).
Pupil of the music school of the said town.
First opera—Venice 1819.
The last—God knows where.
Up to the present I have composed 65—
together with church music, quartets, etc., etc.
A friend of friends—who will always maintain
that he is not concerned with popular
opinion, fortune, himself or low matters.
Widower for two years—sad by nature—not
rich, but without desire for riches.
                    Paris 8th June 1839."[1]

This is how Donizetti described himself, briefly and modestly. At this point in his life he could have boasted truthfully that he was the foremost composer of Italian operas, famous throughout Europe, sought after by the prestigious opera houses of Naples, Vienna, Paris and London. He had composed both comic and tragic operas that were triumphant successes in his time. In fact, these operas have held their place in the active repertoire of major opera companies for more than a century and a half.

In his autobiographical sketch, the expression "etc., etc." includes Donizetti's solo songs and duets, dozens of them. These are not operatic excerpts, but independent pieces with piano accompaniment. Many of them were commercial successes, even internationally, and were sung with delight by professionals and amateurs alike.

This volume brings together a representative collection of Donizetti's songs. Some of them were published in several editions during his lifetime and in the years just following, while others have never been in print. Recent years have brought a revival of interest in Donizetti's songs, but the songs selected here have not been published anywhere else for more than a century.

Donizetti's Life

Gaetano Donizetti, born on November 29, 1797, was modest in writing about himself, but his contemporaries wrote about him in terms of high praise. It was well known that he worked hard; he created over 600 works, including more than 60 operas, in a career of less than 30 years. When he had composed an opera, he also had to teach the music to the singers, rehearse the orchestra, adapt the score to the singers' needs and, finally, conduct at least the first three performances of the new work. In Donizetti's whole career only two of his operas premiered without his personal supervision; both were failures. During rehearsals for an opera, Donizetti was usually negotiating a contract with some other city for his next opera. And at other times he was writing church music, songs, instrumental music— whatever might bring in a regular flow of income between operas.

Although his life was often trying, Donizetti was known for his warmth and charm. He made loyal friends in every city where he worked, perhaps because he was never jealous or mean-spirited toward colleagues or rivals. He was considered to be a man of broad culture, well read and able to converse on many subjects. He was tall and handsome, with chestnut hair and blue eyes. The French musician Adolphe Adam, who composed *Cantique de Noël,* wrote of Donizetti that "it was impossible to be near him without loving him."[2]

This successful and sophisticated musician was born in Bergamo, Italy, which is located 47 km. northeast of Milan. His parents, poor working people, had an apartment below ground level; it was windowless at the front of the house and open to daylight and to a garden only at the back. Two of the six Donizetti children died in infancy; Gaetano was the youngest of the four who survived.

Giovanni Simone Mayr. Donizetti's teacher, Bavarian (German) by birth, is shown here in mid-life, wearing the tousled hair, ruffled tie and heavy coat that were in fashion in the Napoleonic era.

Musical talent must have been latent in the family, as seen in the fact that Gaetano's oldest brother, Giuseppe, also became a professional musician and had an influential career in Turkey. The brothers owed the development of their talent to the musical training offered at the cathedral in their hometown. The music director of the cathedral was an outstanding Bavarian conductor and composer, Johannes Simon Mayr (1763–1845), who Italianized his name to Giovanni Simone Mayr. Mayr founded a charitable school to instruct boys not only to sing in the cathedral choir, but also to play the violin and keyboard. Young Gaetano had some unspecified defect in his voice, but Mayr kept him on at the school and encouraged his musical growth in every possible way. By the age of 13 he had begun to compose. At sixteen the school records show that he sang bass and he even sang a tiny role in a local theater, probably in one of Mayr's operas.

Mayr is largely forgotten now, but he was well known in his time, and Donizetti was proud to identify himself as a student of Mayr's. He encouraged his students to read literary classics and discussed ideas with them, exercising a strong moral and intellectual influence in their lives. When Donizetti was ready to leave Bergamo at seventeen, Mayr wrote letters of recommendation: to the music school at Bologna; to a wealthy patron, asking for financial help; and to the music publisher, Giovanni Ricordi, whom Donizetti met when he passed through Milan.

After only two years of further study in Bologna, Donizetti began to build a career as an opera composer. Just before his 21st birthday he saw the first professional production of one of his operas in Venice. Donizetti composed constantly and efficiently; Mayr had taught him not to use a keyboard when he wrote. In a twelve year period he composed about 30 operas, culminating in *Anna Bolena* (1830, Milan), which is regarded as the first opera of his maturity. He went on to write another 36 operas, including such masterpieces as: *L'Elisir d'amore* (1832, Milan); *Lucia di Lammermoor* (1835, Naples); *La Fille du régiment* (1840, Paris); *La Favorite* (1840, Paris); and *Don Pasquale* (1843, Paris).

Success in Donizetti's career was not accompanied by happiness in his personal life. He fell in love with a beautiful young woman in Rome, Virginia Vasselli; she returned his love and they married in June, 1828. They lived together in Naples, where Donizetti served for ten years as Director of Music of the Royal Theaters of Naples. They had three children, all of whom died before their mother. Virginia, weakened by exhaustion, grief and probably an infectious disease as well, succumbed in July 1837, at the age of 29. In the space of eight years Donizetti lost his father, his mother, two sons, a daughter, and his wife. It is no wonder that he described himself as "sad by nature."

After Virginia's death, Donizetti willingly moved away from Naples. He settled in Paris, where he could produce operas at any of four theaters. He continued to work hard, hoping to retire in financial security. In 1842 *Linda di Chamounix* had great success in Vienna. Donizetti was appointed conductor to the Austrian court, a post that allowed him to spend six months a year in Vienna and six months away. The very next year he began to show signs of irrational behavior, and rumors began to circulate about his failing creativity and lack of self control.

Donizetti suffered from syphilis, a diagnosis that was later confirmed by an autopsy. His mental decline caused him to be placed in a sanatorium near Paris for more than a year. He became paralyzed and nearly unable to speak. Under these difficult circumstances, his nephew managed to remove him from the sanatorium and transport him to Bergamo, where faithful friends cared for him until he died on April 8, 1848.

The Style of Donizetti's Songs

Romanza is the word that Donizetti and his publishers most often used to describe his songs with piano accompaniment. This was the generic term for a lyrical song, usually a love song. Patricia Adkins Chiti has described how the romanza developed as a genre in the early 1800s.[3] Briefly, new techniques of music engraving and printing made it economical to print songs with piano accompaniment, and a new middle class provided an ample market both for pianos and for songs accessible to amateur singers. Donizetti's simpler songs were written for this lucrative market, while his more difficult songs were showpieces fashioned for specific professional singers. Both types include songs of high caliber, which are represented in this collection.

Donizetti's musical language is so familiar to opera lovers that it may seem difficult to recognize the personal and distinctive traits that set him apart from other Italian composers. We can best understand his individuality by comparison with several other composers, two who influenced him and three who did not.

Giovanni Simone Mayr gave Donizetti a musical training that hardly anyone else in Italy could have given him. Mayr studied the works of Haydn, Mozart and Beethoven and conducted them in concerts in which Donizetti participated as a choral singer. Mayr passed on the lessons of the Viennese masters to Donizetti, particularly in three areas:

1) skillful scoring for orchestral wind instruments, which Austrian composers used much more than the Italians;

2) smooth and flexible chromatic modulations, such as the Austrians used in the development sections of sonatas;

3) mastery of the pure forms of instrumental music, used by Donizetti in many works, such as his 16 string quartets.

The first of these areas strengthened Donizetti's operatic scoring, but the other two are relevant also to his songs. With the skills learned from Mayr, Donizetti wrote songs with ingenious modulations and a variety of forms. In this volume are not only strophic songs but examples of strophic variations, rondo form, and through-composed songs, as well as compound forms with sections in contrasting tempos.

Gioacchino Rossini (1792–1868) dominated the operatic world in which Donizetti strove to make his way. At the Italian opera in Paris, for instance, Rossini's works made up about half of the works in the listed repertoire during the 1820s and accounted for about two thirds of the performances given.[4] To survive, Donizetti learned all of Rossini's tricks, even to the point of imitating his famous crescendos. Rossini accomplished one great change that affected all opera: he began to write out all of the vocal ornamentations that he wanted and to forbid his singers to improvise embellishments as Baroque and Classical era singers had done. Rossini did not, however, take up the stylistic challenges of Romanticism. After Rossini composed *Guillaume Tell* (Wilhelm Tell, 1829), he stopped composing operas entirely, rather than progress even further away from his Classical roots. Romanticism shows up in Donizetti's songs in terms of his free use of chromaticism and his choices of a wide variety of subject matter. Rossini would not have been interested in song texts with the sentimentality of *Le petit montagnard* (page 76), the serious historical background of *Giovanna Grey* (page 26), or the downright silliness of *Il Trovatore in caricatura* (page 40).

Franz Schubert (1797–1828), the master with whom all song composers must be compared, was only ten months older than Donizetti. Both musicians were born into poor families and received musical training in choir schools. Schubert never escaped poverty, as Donizetti did. Under Beethoven's influence, Schubert composed in many genres but failed repeatedly in his attempts to compose operas. Equipped with a brilliant piano technique and stimulated by the outpouring of German Romantic poetry, Schubert created a new partnership of equality between piano and voice and thereby changed the history of song. In contrast, Donizetti always focussed attention on the singer and allowed the pianist to do no more than provide an appropriate framework and background to a song.

Vincenzo Bellini (1801–1835) and **Giuseppe Verdi** (1813–1901) were respectively Donizetti's foremost competitor and his foremost successor. Donizetti generously acknowledged both great talents without a trace of jealousy. Superb as Bellini's melodic writing often was, he lacked Donizetti's versatility, particularly his flair for comedy. (Of course, the same criticism might have been made of Verdi if he had not lived to write *Falstaff* at the age of 80.) In Verdi's hands opera became ever grander, using larger orchestras and therefore, larger and larger voices.

Sources of the Songs

All of the songs in this volume were edited on the basis of Donizetti's autograph manuscripts or of early editions.

Donizetti did not date his manuscripts and often gave them away as keepsakes to friends. Because there were no copyright laws, a song that was successful in one city might be published within a few months by rival publishers in other cities, with or without any payment to the composer. The early editions were seldom dated, and it is often unclear which of them came on the market first. To discover and catalog all of the manuscripts and early editions of Donizetti's songs would require years of bibliographical research, a project which no one has yet accomplished.

A significant preliminary list of Donizetti's vocal works is contained in the biography by Herbert Weinstock.[5] He located 208 solo songs and 48 vocal duets, and he offers many details, including names of persons to whom songs were dedicated.

A more extensive song list appears in *New Grove*, apparently compiled by the authors of the biographical article, William Ashbrook and Julian Budden.[6] That list builds on Weinstock's but gives few details about individual works.

Another listing of Donizetti songs appears in an Italian music encyclopedia that is known by UTET, the acronym of its publisher.[7] No name is given for the author of the biographical article nor the compiler of the song list, which includes 11 collections of songs and 270 individual titles of songs and duets.

I am indebted to all three lists for valuable information. Throughout this book they are referred to respectively by the names Weinstock, New Grove and UTET.

The introductory notes to each song state the exact source from which it was taken. In some cases the publisher of the song cannot be identified because the name was cut off in the process of binding. The library where each song was found is identified by its city, as follows:

Cambridge, Massachusetts: Eda Kuhn Loeb Music Library, Harvard University;

New Haven, Connecticut: Yale University Library;

Milan: Biblioteca del Conservatorio di Musica 'Giuseppe Verdi';

New York, New York: The Pierpont Morgan Library;

Paris: Bibliothèque Nationale;

Rome: Biblioteca musicale governativa del Conservatorio di Musica 'S. Cecilia'.

"My portrait made by myself." A caricature, signed and dated 1841. The original is in the Museo Donizettiano, Bergamo.

1. Translated by John Allitt in *Donizetti and the Tradition of Romantic Love* (London: Donizetti Society, 1975).

2. Adolphe Adam, *Derniers souvenirs d'un musicien* (Paris, 1857).

3. Patricia Adkins Chiti, *Italian Art Songs of the Romantic Era* (Van Nuys, CA: Alfred Publishing Co., 1994).

4. Patrick Barbier, *Opera in Paris, 1800–1850: a lively history,* translated by Robert Luoma (Portland, OR: Amadeus Press, 1995).

5. Herbert Weinstock, *Donizetti and the World of Opera in Italy, Paris, and Vienna in the First Half of the Nineteenth Century* (New York: Pantheon Books, 1963).

6. *New Grove Dictionary of Music and Musicians* (London: Macmillan Publishers Limited, 1980).

7. *Dizionario enciclopedico universale della musica e dei musicisti* (Turin: Unione Tipografico-Editrice Torinese, 1985).

About This Edition

Because these 20 songs come from manuscripts and from various publishers in several countries, it is necessary to impose some uniformity on them without altering them in any significant way. For instance, modern clefs are used, small note values are beamed together, and obvious misprints have been corrected without any special notice.

In manuscripts and editions from the 1800s slurs are used sporadically to indicate a specific phrasing, a generalized legato style, or sometimes a portamento between two notes. Such slurs are reproduced in this volume with dotted lines. Normal solid slurs are used to show that a syllable is carried from one note to another in a melisma.

Ornamental notes are reproduced exactly as in the sources. Wherever there could be suspicion that they are not correct, a footnote has been added to say what the correct interpretation may be. It is *not* advisable to improvise additional ornaments in these songs. Donizetti wrote as much ornamentation as is needed.

Song texts have also been edited for uniformity. Spelling and punctuation are modernized. In many cases the original edition distributed text syllables under notes carelessly, resulting in inappropriate accentuation. Native Italian singers would simply correct such errors at sight, as they have been corrected here.

Italian publishers differ on the question of whether to capitalize the first word of a line of verse. The choice made here is to do so when the text is printed in verse form, but not when the text is printed with music.

Joan Thompson, my wife, shared in the excitement of discovering these songs and spent hours in Paris and Rome copying scores by hand when we were not allowed to photocopy them. I thank her for her boundless enthusiasm and understanding. As always, I thank my capable and creative colleagues at Alfred Publishing Co.

John Glenn Paton
Los Angeles

"Se a te d'intorno scherza." *The opening measures of the autograph copy owned by The Pierpont Morgan Library, New York. The tempo marking,* Andante sostenuto, *is abbreviated. The voice part, marked* Canto, *is in soprano clef. The piano part is marked* Pia. *The notes that make up the left-hand chords are not always vertically aligned.*

*"Le petit montagnard." This sentimental lithograph appeared on the cover
of the sheet music published by B. Schott, Mainz.*

Amiamo

[amˈjaːmo]

(Let's love!)

or ke lleta neinviːta
1 **Or che l'età ne invita,**
Now that the-age to-it invites,

ʧerkjaːmo di godeːr
2 **Cerchiamo di goder.**
let-us-seek to be-happy.

listante del pjaʧeːr paːsːa e non tɔrna
3 **L'istante del piacer passa e non torna.**
The-moment of pleasure passes and does-not return.

graːve divjɛːn la viːta
4 **Grave divien la vita**
Serious becomes the life

se nnon si kɔʎː ʎeil fjoːr
5 **Se non si coglie il fior;**
if not one gathers the flower.

di freske rɔːzeamoːr soːlo ladɔrna
6 **Di fresche rose amor solo l'adorna.**
With fresh roses love only it-adorns.

pju bbɛlːa sɛi pju ddeːviad
7 **Più bella sei, più devi**
More beautiful you-are, more you-owe

amoːr voːti e fe
8 **Ad amor voti e fé;**
to love vows and faith;

altra beltaː non ɛ keun suo tribuːto
9 **Altra beltà non è che un suo tributo.**
Another beauty naught is but a his tribute.

amjaːm kei di son brɛːvi
10 **Amiam ché i dì son brevi;**
Let-us-love, because the days are brief.

ɛun ʤorno sɛntsamoːre
11 **È un giorno senza amore**
Is a day without love

un ʤorno di doloːr ʤorno perduːto
12 **Un giorno di dolor, giorno perduto.**
a day of sadness, day lost.

Poetic idea: "Let us be happy while we can! Gather the flowers and spend today in love!"

Donizetti had a friend, Giovanni Agostino Perotti, who was the music director of the famous St. Mark's Cathedral in Venice. Although Perotti was 28 years older than Donizetti, they enjoyed a hearty friendship. Weinstock says: "A group of warm, humorous, admiring letters that Donizetti wrote him was obtained for Verdi's autograph collection."

The sheet music of this charming and lively song bears a dedication "to the very dear daughter of the very dear and very brilliant Perotti." Unfortunately, her name is not given.

It is not known when this song was composed, but Donizetti visited the Perotti family in Venice in December 1837.

Source: *Gazzetta Musicale di Milano,* Year 23, number 10 (Milan: Ricordi, ca. 1865). Copy in Rome. Original key: D major. UTET says that this song was published posthumously in *Primavera a Sorrento* (Springtime in Sorrento) (Naples: Cottrau, 1871), but the Ricordi publication appears to be earlier.

Amiamo

Eliz. Parcells - YouTube

Poet unknown

Gaetano Donizetti

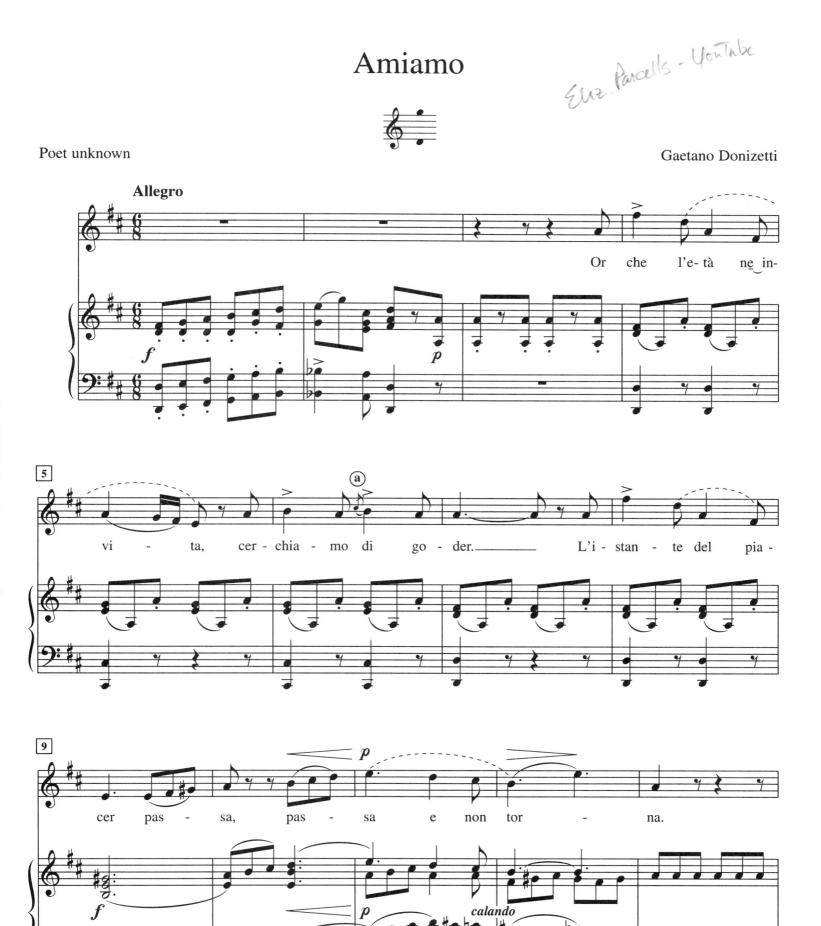

Or che l'e- tà ne in-
vi - ta, cer chia - mo di go- der._____ L'i - stan - te del piacer pas - sa, pas- sa e non tor - na.

ⓐ All grace notes in this song are to be performed quickly and before the beat.

Literal translation: Because our youth invites us to do so, let us look for happiness. An instant of pleasure passes and does not come back.

Life becomes solemn if one does not gather its flowers; only love can adorn life with fresh roses.

The more lovely you are, the more you owe vows and fidelity to love. There is no other suitable offering to bring to love.

Let's love, for the days are brief. A day without love is a day of sadness, a wasted day.

Stanza 2: Shepherd, if you want to sigh of love to your shepherdess, there are no secrets here; we love without hypocrisy.

Stanza 3: And you, beautiful Lisette with your pretty flock, do not go away alone just as night is falling here under the elms.

meau, il_ fait nuit sous_ l'or - meau._ Au tic - tac des ca - sta - gnet - tes, au

son du cha - lu - meaux, chan - tez, dan - sez, fil - let - tes, sous ces verts or -

meaux. Tic - tac, dan - sez, tic - tac, chan - tez, fil - let - tes, fil - let - tes, chan - tez, dan _

sez sous_ ces verts or - meaux, sous_ ces verts_ or - meaux.

Berceuse

[bɛr søz]

1
kwesto mio fiʎːʎoɛun fjorelːliːn damoːre
Questo mio figlio è un fiorellin d'amore
This my son is a little-flower of-love

2
ke pper kandoːre non la tʃɛːdeal dʒiʎːʎo
Che per candore non la cede al giglio.
that for whiteness not it concedes to-the lily.

3 **È un fiorellin d'amor questo mio figlio**

4 **Che al giglio non la cede per candore.**

5
la ninːnananːna kon la voːtʃe santa
La ninna-nanna con la voce santa
The lullaby with the voice holy

6
te la kanta dal tʃɛːlo la madonːna
Te la canta dal cielo la Madonna:
to-you it sings from Heaven the Madonna:

7
dormi dormi andʒoletːto mio
Dormi, dormi, angioletto mio...
Sleep, sleep, dear-angel mine...

8
in kwesto tʃɛːl di dio non vɛuna stelːla
In questo ciel di Dio non v'è una stella
In this Heaven of God not there-is a star

9
ke ddiːka soːn pju bbɛlːlal fiʎːʎo mio
Che dica: son più bella al figlio mio;
that could-say, "I-am more beautiful," to son my.

10 **Non v'è una stella in questo ciel di Dio**

11
keal fiʎːʎo mio pwɔ ddir io soːn pju bbɛlːla
Che al figlio mio può dir: io son più bella...
that to son mine can say, "I am more beautiful...

12
non vɛ nnel paradiːzo un kerubiːno
Non v'è nel paradiso un cherubino
Not there-is in Paradise a little-angel

13
keal mio bambiːno rasːsomiʎːʎin viːzo
Che al mio bambino rassomigli in viso.
that to my baby could-resemble in face.

14 **Un cherubin non v'è nel paradiso**

15 **Che rassomigli in viso al mio bambino.**

Poetic idea: "No other mother's baby is as wonderful as mine!"

Donizetti gave this lullaby a playful setting in a tempo and rhythm that resemble a Spanish bolero. The poet was also playful, taking the first couplet of each stanza and rearranging the words to make the second couplet. The resulting song may be a lullaby, but it is even more a character study of the mother who sings it: she is proud, lively, humorous, devoted to the Virgin Mary, and totally in love with her baby boy.

In performance, notice that the fermata in measure 17 is over the rest; the note before the rest should not be lengthened. Also, the fermata should not add more than one half beat to the length of the measure.

Line 9 originally read: *Che dica: io son...* The pronoun, which creates a difficult triphthong, is not essential to the meaning and may be omitted: *Che dica: son...*

Source: *"Berceuse"* (Paris: n.p., n.d.) Copy in Paris, A.8615. Original key: B-flat minor.

The source copy has no cover and no publisher's name, but it was engraved in Paris by a company identified in small type. UTET says that the song was published posthumously in *Album du Gaulois,* 1869, and the source copy may be identical with that publication.

The text underlay in the second and third stanzas is incorrect because the engraver did not know which Italian syllables should be on stressed beats.

In the source copy the poet is identified as Achille de Lauzières, but this seems to be an error. He was the poet of a different *"Berceuse"* by Donizetti with a French text. If a French version of this song had existed, the Parisian publisher would have used it. In my opinion, this poem is an Italian original, not a translation.

Berceuse

Poet unknown

Gaetano Donizetti

Que - sto mio fi - glio è un
In que - sto ciel di

fio - rel - lin d'a - mo - re che per can-do - re
Dio non_v'è u - na stel - la che di - ca: son più

Literal translation: 1) This son of mine is a little love-flower that is whiter

2) In God's heaven there is not one star that could claim to be more

(1) than any lily. In heaven the Madonna is singing a lullaby for you with her holy voice. Sleep, my little angel.
(2) beautiful than my son.

mi - o. La nin - na - nan - na la Ma - dɔn - na dal___ ciɛ - lo te la

can - ta, dal ciɛ - lo___ te la can - ta.

Non v'ɛ̀ nel pa - ra - di - so un che - ru -

There's not a cherub in Paradise

with a face like my baby's.

55

mi - o. La nin - na - nan - na la Ma - don - na dal___ cie - lo te la

59

can - ta, dal cie - lo___ te la can - ta.

A sample of Donizetti's handwriting. In 1833 Donizetti wrote to his librettist, Felice Romani, requesting alterations to the libretto of an opera, Rosmonda d'Inghilterra. *This is the conclusion of the letter, translated: "The Introduction shorter if possible. And whatever pleases my friend Romani to do for us or to delete for us—Donizetti."*

Giovanna Grey
[dʒovanːa grɛi]

(Lady Jane Grey)

io morːrɔ̣ sonaːta ɛ lloːra
1 Io morrò; sonata è l'ora.
I shall-die; sounded has the-hour.

oɲːɲi pja̱nto amiːko ɛ vvaːno
2 Ogni pianto amico è vano.
Every weeping friendly is vain.

dun karnɛːfitʃe la maːno
3 D'un carnefice la mano
Of-an executioner the hand

la tu̱a spɔːza tokːkera̱
4 La tua sposa toccherà…
the your wife will-touch…

non aŋkoːr mi kompje il soːle
5 Non ancor mi compie il sole
Not again for-me finishes the sun

di noˈvanːni il dopːpjo dʒiːro
6 Di nov'anni il doppio giro,
of nine-years the double revolution,

e nnel puːro adːdzurːro empiːro
7 E nel puro azzurro empiro
and in-the pure blue sky

pju pper me non brilːlera̱
8 Più per me non brillerà.
more for me not it-will-shine.

il su̱o radːdʒo io saluta̱i
9 Il suo raggio io salutai
The its ray I greeted

fra lle nebːbje matːtutiːne
10 Fra le nebbie mattutine,
amid the mists of-morning,

ne vvedrɔ̣lːlo sul konfiːne
11 Né vedrollo sul confine
nor I-shall-see-it on-the limit

delːle tɛːnebre del diˑ
12 Delle tenebre del dì.
of-the-shadows of-the day.

ma ttu puːr kwaˑl fjoːr naʃːʃɛnte
13 Ma tu pur, qual fior nascente,
But you only, that flower being-born,

mjeter a̱ la riˑa kondanːna
14 Mieterà la ria condanna;
will-reap the guilty condemnation

lamorɔːza tu̱a dʒovanːna
15 L'amorosa tua Giovanna
the-loving your Jane

trista dɔːte aimɛ tofːfri
16 Trista dote, ahimè, t'offrì.
sad dowry, alas, to-you-offered.

volutːta luzi̱nge onori
17 Voluttà, lusinghe, onori,
Delights, flatteries, honors,

doːveandaːr doːvɛ kwel trɔːno
18 Dove andar? Dov'è quel trono,
where did-they-go? Where-is that throne,

ke ddi sɔrte infa̱usto doːno
19 Che di sorte infausto dono,
that, of fate unfavorable gift,

fumːmo spinti a kkalpestaːr
20 Fummo spinti a calpestar.
we-were forced to trample-on.

kwaːzi polve al turbo iraːto
21 Quasi polve al turbo irato,
Like dust to-the-whirlwind stirred-up,

tutːto fudːdʒe e a me sinvoːla
22 Tutto fugge e a me s'invola,
everything flees and to me vanishes,

ma̱unimːmaːdʒine la soːla
23 Ma un'immagine è la sola
but one-image is the only-one

ke mmi dʒundʒe a konturbaːr
24 Che mi giunge a conturbar.
that to-me comes to perturb.

tu mintɛndi ea̱l punto estrɛːmo
25 Tu m'intendi, e al punto estremo
You me-understand, and at-the point last

vwɔi tornaːr fra lle mie bratːtʃa
26 Vuoi tornar fra le mie braccia:
you-want to-return to the my arms;

a da me bɛːn mio diskatːtʃa
27 Ah! da me, ben mio, discaccia
Ah, from me, dear mine, drive-away

kwesta la̱rva di pjatʃeːr
28 Questa larva di piacer.
this dream of pleasure.

dɔnːna̱io soːn ti pɛrdo e mɔːro
29 Donna io son, ti perdo e moro
Lady I am, you I-lose, and I-die

nelːle̱ta delːla spera̱ntsa
30 Nell'età della speranza.
at-an-age of hope.

	de	mi	laʃ:ʃa	la	kostantsa
31	**Deh,**	**mi**	**lascia**	**la**	**costanza**
	Please,	me	leave	the	faithfulness

	ke	bizoɲ:ɲa	al	mio	kade:r
32	**Che**	**bisogna**	**al**	**mio**	**cader.**
	that	is-needed	at	my	fall.

	strindʒe	il	tɛmpo	i	twɔi	pensjɛːri
33	**Stringe**	**il**	**tempo. I**		**tuoi**	**pensieri**
	Hurries	the	time. The		your	thoughts

	tɔʎːʎi	a	me	rivɔldʒi	al	tʃɛːlo
34	**Togli**	**a**	**me, rivolgi**		**al**	**cielo.**
	take-away	from	me, re-direct		to	Heaven.

	dʒa	per	nɔi	si	skwartʃail	vɛːlo
35	**Già**	**per noi si**			**squarcia il**	**velo**
	Already	for us	itself		rips-open the	veil

	ke	nnaskonde	lavːveniːr
36	**Che**	**nasconde**	**l'avvenir.**
	that	hides	the-future.

	fɔrte	ai	lalma	e	puːro	il	kɔːre
37	**Forte**	**hai**	**l'alma**	**e**	**puro**	**il**	**core,**
	Strong	you-have	the-soul	and	pure	the	heart;

	sarai	priːmo	adːdiːo	minseɲːɲa
38	**Sarai**	**primo,**	**addio.**	**M'insegna**
	you-will-be	first.	Farewell.	Me-teach

	koːme	dɛbːba	di	te	deɲːɲa
39	**Come**	**debba,**	**de**	**te**	**degna,**
	how	I-ought,	of	you	worthy,

	sul	patiːbolo	saliːr
40	**Sul**	**patibolo**	**salir.**
	to-the	gallows	climb.

Poetic idea: "Forget my fate, and turn your thoughts towards Heaven."

This song portrays a young noblewoman who is facing a tragic death. At sixteen years of age Lady Jane Grey was Queen of England for nine days. Within a year she was beheaded, a pathetic victim of political forces far beyond her control.

The great question of Jane's time was religion. The Reformation was underway in Europe. King Henry VIII, Jane's great-uncle, had declared the Church of England to be independent from the Roman Catholic Church. At stake were matters of faith, political power, and large tracts of land that belonged to monasteries. When Henry died, he left only one son, Edward VI, a nine-year-old boy. Edward was sickly and died at age 15 of tuberculosis. The crown should

have passed directly to his sister Mary Tudor, a Catholic, but Protestant leaders feared losing power if she led England back to the Catholic Church. To prevent this from happening, Edward decreed that his successors should be Lady Jane Grey and her male heirs, putting her ahead of his two sisters, Mary and Elizabeth. The advisor who induced Edward to do this also arranged the marriage of his own son, Lord Guildford Dudley, to Jane on May 21, 1553. She went to live with the Dudley family, whom she disliked, and had a nervous breakdown.

When Edward VI died in July 1553, Jane was proclaimed queen, although she fainted when the idea was first proposed to her. The people, however, supported the claim of Mary Tudor, and after nine days Jane gave up the crown voluntarily. Nevertheless, in November she and her husband were arraigned on charges of high treason. She plead guilty and both were beheaded on February 12, 1554. History records that she went to her death without tears or protests, and the people of England remembered her with sympathy.

Donizetti apparently had a great interest in British history, borne out by his three operas about queens: Anne Boleyn, the second wife of Henry VIII (*Anna Bolena*); Anne Boleyn's daughter, Elizabeth I (*Elisabetta, Regina d'Inghilterra*); and Elizabeth's rival, Mary Stuart, Queen of Scotland (*Maria Stuarda*).

In measure 20 a phrasing problem occurs that also occurs often in the operas of Verdi: the natural, logical opportunity for breathing, between beats 2 and 3, is apparently prevented by the slur that covers the whole measure. The only possible solution is that the slur is an expressive one and that the singer must energetically maintain the continuity of the musical expression while taking the breath that is needed.

Line 4: *la tua sposa* refers to Jane herself, and the poem as a whole is addressed to her husband, Lord Dudley.

Line 13: *qual fior nascente* refers to Lord Dudley as being still in the flower of his youth. This and following lines probably idealize Jane's marriage, which was primarily political rather than romantic.

Source: *Tre melodie postume* (Three posthumous songs) (Chiasso: L'Euterpe Ticinese, no date). Copy in Milan. Key: F minor. The title is misspelled as "*Giovanna Gray*." No poet is named. A German translation is given.

UTET states that "*Giovanna Gray*" was first published in *Fiori di sepolcro* (Napoli: Girard, no date), but I have not seen that edition.

Giovanna Grey

Poet unknown

Gaetano Donizetti

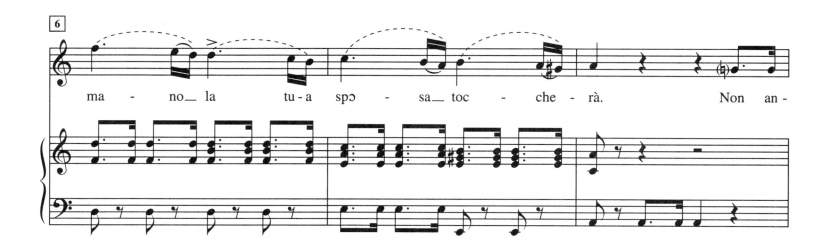

Literal translation: 1) I shall die; the hour has already sounded. The weeping of my friends is in vain. An executioner's hand will touch your wife.

The sun will not finish eighteen cycles for me, and will shine no more for me in the pure blue sky. I greeted the sun through morning mists, but I shall not see it pass into evening.

Ma tu pur, qual fior na - scen - te, mie - te - rà la ri - a con - dan - na; l'a - mo - ro - sa tua Gio - van - na tri - sta do - te, ahi - mè, t'of - frì. Vo - lut - tà, lu - sin - ghe, o - no - ri, do - ve an - dar? Do - v'è quel tro - no, che di

2) Only you, young flower still opening, are condemned along with me; your loving Jane brought you a sad dowry, alas! Luxury, flattery, honor—where have they gone? Where is that throne, given

sor - te in-fau - sto— do - no, fum-mo— spin - ti a cal - pe - star. Qua - si— pol - ve al tur - bo i - ra - to, tut - to— fug - ge— e a me s'in - vo - la, ma u - n'im - ma - gi - ne è la so - la che mi giun - ge— a— con - tur - bar.

to us by an unhappy fate, that we were forced to reject with scorn? Like dust picked up by a whirlwind, everything has flown away and vanished. Only one image remains to disturb me.

3) You understand me, and at the hour of death you ask to be in my arms again; ah, my dear, forget this dream of pleasure. I marry, I lose you, and I die, all at an age that should be full of hope. Please,

la - scia_la co - stan - za che_bi - so - gna al mio ca -

der. Strin-ge il tem - po. I_tuoi pen - sie - ri to - gli a

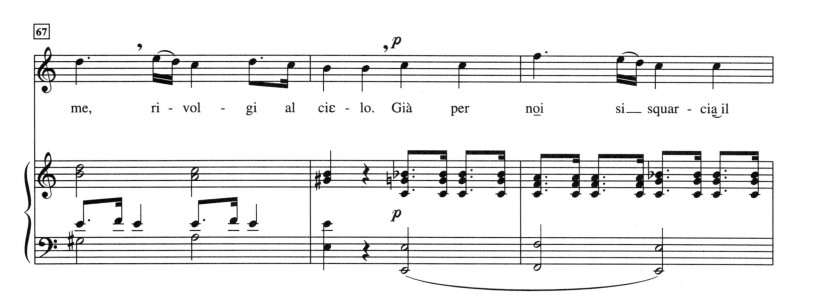

me, ri - vol - gi al cie - lo. Già per noi si_squar - cia il

be faithful to me, as I require at the time of my fall. Time flies. Turn your thoughts away from me and toward Heaven.
For us the veil

that conceals the future is beginning to part. You have a strong soul and pure heart. You will go first—farewell. Show me how to be worthy of you as I climb to the gallows. Farewell.

Il giglio e la rosa

(The lily and the rose)

[il dʒiʎːʎo e la rɔːza]

1 **Non sdegnar, vezzosa Irene,**
non zdeɲːɲaːr vetːtsoːza ireːne
Not scorn, lovely Irene,

2 **Questo giglio e questa rosa,**
kwesto dʒiʎːʎoe kkwesta rɔːza
this lily and this rose

3 **Che l'aurora rugiadosa**
ke llaurɔːra rudʒadoːza
that the-dawn rosy

4 **Di sue stille inumidì.**
di sue stilːle inumidi
with its dewdrops moistened.

5 **L'uno è fior sacro ad Imene,**
lunoɛ ffjoːr saːkroad imeːne
The-one is flower sacred to Hymen,

6 **L'altro piacque al dio bendato:**
laltro pjakːkwe al dio bendaːto
the-other pleases to-the god blindfolded.

7 **Ambo nacquero in un prato,**
ambo nakːkweɾo in un praːto
Both were-born in one meadow,

8 **Ed un rivo ambo nudrì.**
ed un riːvo ambo nudri
and one river both nourished.

9 **L'uno è figlio del pudore,**
lunoɛ ffiʎːʎo del pudoːre
The-one is son of modesty,

10 **A beltade è l'altro caro,**
a bbeltaːde llaltro kaːro
to beauty is the-other dear,

11 **Ed olezzano del paro**
ed oledːdzano del paːɾo
and they-are-fragrant of equally

12 **Ed han regno in ogni cor.**
ed an reɲːɲo in oɲːŋi kɔːr
and have rule in every heart.

13 **L'un tu vinci nel candore**
lun tu vintʃi nel kandoːɾe
The-one you defeat in-the whiteness

14 **Del tuo seno e del tuo volto,**
del tuo seːno e del tuo vɔlto
of your bosom and of your face;

15 **Ogni pregio all'altro è tolto**
oɲːɲi predʒoalːlaltro ɛ ttɔlto
every prize from-the-other is taken-away

16 **Dal tuo labbro incantator.**
dal tuo labːbro iŋkantatoːr
by your mouth enchanting.

Poetic idea: "Lovely Irene, this lily and this rose are my gifts to you, one as white as your skin, the other as red as your lips."

For these words, as conventional and sweet as a Valentine card, Donizetti provided music of charm and simplicity.

Even if one recognizes that this is perhaps Donizetti's shortest and simplest song, it is also an excellent example of *bel canto* vocal style. Notice the variety of articulation that is required: *legato* as the normal manner; a quick, light *acciaccatura* in measure 2; an unexpected *staccato* on beat 1 and an *accento* on beat 2 of measure 3; an expressive *appoggiatura* in measure 10. In measure 13 the singer builds to a *forte* tone on a *fermata* and then, without breathing, continues singing the next phrase in a *piano* dynamic. The singer who can do all of this well has learned a great deal of vocal technique.

Source: This is the first song in *Raccolta di canzonette e duettini italiani, napoletani e francesi* (Collection of songs and duets in Italian, Neapolitan and French) (Milano: F. Lucca, no date). Copy at Milan. Original key: G major.

This volume was discussed on page 14 with the reasons why it was probably published no later than 1833. This song is one of those with the voice part notated in soprano clef, which has a somewhat old-fashioned look for the period. UTET identifies the poet as Pietro Metastasio (1698–1782), but I have been unable to find the poem among his works.

Il giglio e la rosa

Pietro Metastasio (?)

Gaetano Donizetti

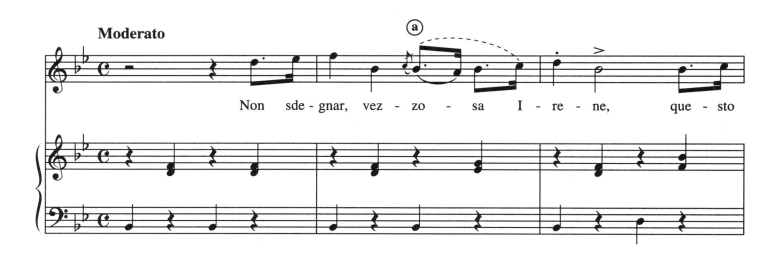

Non sde - gnar, vez - zo - sa I - re - ne, que - sto

gi - glio e que - sta ro - sa, che l'au - ro - ra ru - gia -

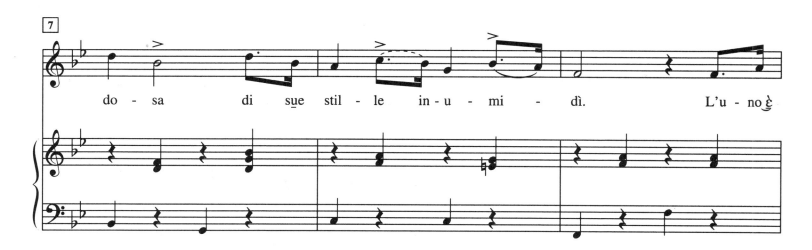

do - sa di sue stil - le in - u - mi - dì. L'u - no è

ⓐ Sing the acciaccatura lightly and before the beat.

Literal translation: 1) Lovely Irene, do not be scornful of this lily and this rose, that still have morning dew on them.

(b) Accent the appoggiatura; sing it and the quarter note both as eighth notes.

One is the favorite flower of the god of marriage and the other of the god of love.
Both sprang up in the same meadow and were watered by the same stream.

2) One flower is the emblem of modesty and the other of beauty; they both are fragrant and they both rule
  every heart. You surpass the lily by the whiteness of your bosom and your

vol - to, o - gni pre - gio al - l'al - tro è _____ tɔl - to dal tuo

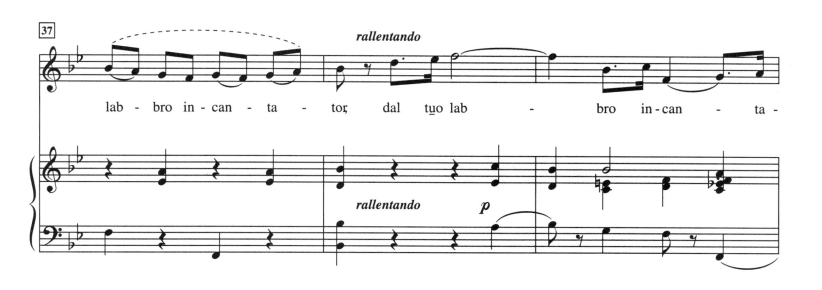

lab - bro in - can - ta - tor, dal tuo lab - bro in - can - ta -

tor, dal tuo lab - bro in - can - ta - tor.

face; your enchanting lips take every prize that belonged to the rose.

Il trovatore in caricatura (The silly troubadour)

[il trovatoːre in karikatuːra]

1
eːra   nɔtːte   lla   kampaːna
Era   notte   e   la   campana
It-was   night   and   the   bell

2
daːvaun tokːkoɲːɲi sekondo dɔn   dɔn
Dava un   tocco ogni   secondo—don,   don.
gave a   stroke every   second,   dong,   dong.

3
gratʃidaːr   sudia   la   raːna
Gracidar   s'udia   la   rana
Croaking   was-heard   the   frog

4
del   pantaːno nel   profondo kra   kra
Del   pantano   nel   profondo—crà, crà.
of-the   marsh   at-the   bottom,   croak.

5
il   kjaroːr   di   mɛsta   luːna
Il   chiaror   di   mesta   luna
The   light   of   sad   moon

6
rifletːteːa   sulːla   laguːna
Riflettea   sulla   laguna,
reflected   on-the   lagoon

7
alːlorke   dʒunseal   kastɛlːlo
Allorché   giunse   al   castello
when   approached to-the   castle

8
il   meskiːno   trovatoːr
Il   meschino   trovator.
the   miserable   troubador.

9
ma   trovɔ   kjuːzoil   kantʃɛlːlo
Ma   trovò   chiuso il   cancello,
But   he-found   closed the   gate,

10
ɛːran   tutːtin   lɛtːtoalːloːr
Eran   tutti in   letto allor.
they-were   all   in   bed   already.

11
ɔːza   ʎʎɔkːkiapːpenaestɔrːre
Osa   gli   occhi appena estorre
He-dares   the   eyes   hardly   turn-aside,

12
il   fiʎːʎwɔl   delːla   ʃʃaguːra
Il   figliuol   della   sciagura;
the   son   of   calamity;

13
veːdei   mɛrli   delːla   torːre
Vede i   merli   della   torre,
he-sees the   battlements   of-the   tower,

14
del   verɔn   veːde   le   muːra
Del   veron   vede   le   mura,
of-the   loggia   he-sees   the   walls,

15
ed   aʃːʃɛnder   su   pe   veːtri
Ed   ascender   su   pe'   vetri
and   rising   up   through   windows,

16
veːdei   lemuːrie   ʎʎi   spɛtːtri
Vede i   lemuri e   gli   spettri.
he-sees the   ghosts   and   the   specters.

17
veːdeun   gatːto   soriaːno
Vede   un   gatto   soriano
He-sees   a   cat   tabby

18
ke   korːreva su   e   ddʒu   ɲao
Che   correva   su   e   giù— gnao.
that   ran   up   and   down, meow.

19
ed   un   ombra   di   lontaːno
Ed   un   ombra   di   lontano
And   a   shadow   from   far-away

20
ʎi   pareːa dun   tal   che   ffu
Gli   parea   d'un   tal   che   fù.
to-him   seemed   of-a   person who   was.

21
rifiniːto   dal   viadːdʒo
Rifinito   dal   viaggio
Worn-out   from-the   journey,

22
mɔːvei   pasːsi   lɛnti   lɛnti
Move   i   passi   lenti   lenti
he-moves the   steps   slow,   slow,

23
alːla   kjɛːza   del   vilːladːdʒo
Alla   chiesa   del   villaggio
to-the   church   of-the   village

24
in   frai   saːlitʃi   pjandʒenti
In   fra   i   salici   piangenti,
in   among   the   willows   weeping,

25
e   lla   kroːtʃein   suo   pensjɛːro
E   la   croce   in   suo   pensiero
and   the   cross   in   his   thought

26
salutɔ   del   tʃimitɛːro
Salutò   del   cimitero.
he-greeted   from-the   cemetery.

27
aː   zventuːra   batːteinvaːno
Ah, sventura!   Batte   invano,
Ah, misfortune!   He-knocks in-vain,

28
kjedeinvan   la   karita
Chiede   invan   la   carità,
he-asks   in-vain   the   charity,

29
ke   rispɔndeil   sagrestaːno
Ché   risponde il   sagrestano,
because   answers the   sacristan,

30
il   kuraːto   non   tʃi   sta
"Il   curato   non   ci   sta."
"The   curate   not   there   is."

ɛːɾa   nɔtːted   il   meskiːno
31 Era   notte ed   il   meschino
It-was   night and   the   miserable-one

staːvain   mɛdːdʑo   delːla   viːa
32 Stava in   mezzo   della   via,
stood in   middle   of-the   road,

e   lla   kampaːna   feːa   dɔn   dɔn
33 E   la   campana   fea   don,   don.
and   the   bell   made   dong,   dong.

sɛntsail   bɛkːko   dun   kwatriːno
34 Senza il   becco   d'un   quatrino
Without   the   beak   of-a   penny

per   andaːɾeːalːlosteriːa
35 Per   andare   all'osteria,
to   go   to-the-restaurant,

e   lla   raːna   feːa   kra   kra
36 E   la   rana   fea   crà,   crà.
and   the   frog   made   croak.

non   aveːa   trovaːtoun   kaːne
37 Non   avea   trovato un   cane
Not   he-had   found   a   dog

ke   ʎʎi   desːse   alːlɔdːdʑo   o   ppaːne
38 Che gli   desse   alloggio   o   pane,
that   to-him   would-have-given   lodging   or   bread;

ondeil   miːzeɾo   laŋgwɛnte
39 Onde   il   misero   languente
so-that the   poor-guy   suffering

ditʃeːa   preːzo   dal   dolor
40 Dicea   preso   dal   dolor,
said,   seized   by   sorrow,

se   nnon   pɔsːso   trovar   njɛnte
41 "Se   non   posso   trovar   niente,
"If   not   I-can   find   anything,

perke   ffatːtʃo   il   trovatoːr
42 Perché   faccio   il   trovator?"
Why   am-I-acting   the   troubadour?"

Poetic idea: What could be more pathetically ridiculous than a serenader who goes out at night to sing and finds no one to sing for?

The poor fellow in this song goes first to a local castle, perhaps imagining a fair lady far above his station in life. Unsuccessful at the castle, he knocks at a priest's door, thinking to get a little food, but he is turned away there, too. When we last see him he is standing in the middle of the road, hungry and penniless.

His last question contains a play on words that can hardly be translated into English. *Trovatore* comes from *trovare,* to find or to compose, in the sense of a person's discovering rhymes and poetic combinations of words. In Italian, *trovatore* has both the simple meaning of "finder" and the special meaning of a person who makes up songs

and sings them. That is why our hero makes the sad realization that there is no use being a troubadour if he is not finding food or anything else.

This song was contained in a collection called *Un hiver à Paris* (A Winter in Paris), although none of the songs contains any reference to Paris or to France. Donizetti had previously published in 1836 a set of songs and duets called *Nuits d'été à Pausillipe* (Summer Nights at Posilippo) and in 1837 another collection called *Soirées d Automne à l'Infrascata* (Autumn Evenings at Infrascata). Both Posilippo and Infrascata were picturesque rural villages near Naples in Donizetti's time, but Naples has grown to absorb them into the urban area. The title of the third collection, *Un hiver à Paris,* recognizes that Donizetti no longer spends the winter opera season in Italy. The fact that all three collections were published in Italy with French titles reflects the prestige and stylishness of the French language at the time.

The Italian word *caricare* has several meanings, one of which is "to exaggerate." From this comes the word *caricatura* and the English word "caricature," meaning humor through exaggeration.

Line 34: *Senza il becco d'un quatrino* is an untranslatable idiom that means "without a penny."

Sources: (1) *Un hiver à Paris* (Naples: B. Girard, no date); copy at Rome. Dedicated to the singer Giorgio (here called Georges) Ronconi. (2) *Rêveries napolitaines* (Milan: F. Lucca, no date); copy at Milan. Original key: G minor. Source (1) contains four songs and a duet; source (2) adds another song in two versions, one in Italian and one in French.

Weinstock (page 141) writes about Donizetti in the autumn of 1838: "He also established contact with the music publisher Bernard Lafitte, turning over to him, for a fee of twenty-one hundred francs, six ballate that he had composed in Naples for voice and piano and adding a seventh to make a collection that was published as *Un hiver à Paris ou Rêveries napolitaines.*"

In this pre-copyright period there was no problem for Donizetti in signing a contract in Paris to publish music that had already been published in Naples. The seventh song to which Weinstock refers is probably the French version referred to in source (2).

Based on the evidence above, it seems that the Naples edition appeared in 1838, the Paris edition in early 1839 and the Milan edition a few months later.

The full title of this collection in English would be *A Winter in Paris, or Neapolitan Reveries, a new song album that is a successor to Summer Nights at Posilippo and to Autumn Evenings at Infrascata.*

The dedicatee, Giorgio Ronconi, was a leading baritone who sang premieres of many of Donizetti's operas between 1832 and 1843. In 1842 he sang the title role in Verdi's *Nabucco* and influenced Verdi's concept of the baritone voice. If this song was written for him to sing, his tessitura was exceptionally high.

Il trovatore in caricatura

L. Borsini

Gaetano Donizetti

Literal translation: It was night, and a bell tolled every second—dong, dong. Frogs were croaking in the

44 ■ *Il trovatore in caricatura*

deep marsh—croak, croak. Sad moonlight was reflected on the lagoon as a poor troubadour
approached the castle. But he found the gate locked; everyone was already in bed.

He hardly dared look around him, poor fellow. He saw the battlements of the tower, the walls of the fortifications, and through open windows he could see ghosts and specters rising. He saw a

tabby cat that ran up and down—meow, meow—and from far away he thought he saw the ghost
of someone he had known! Worn out from his venture, he walked with slow steps to the

village church surrounded by weeping willows, and mentally saluted the cross as he passed
through the cemetery. Bad luck! He knocked in vain, for the sacristan responded,

"The priest is not here!" It was night, and the poor fellow stood in the middle of the road,
and the bell rang, without a penny in his pocket to go to a tavern, and the frog croaked.

He had not even found a dog that would give him lodging or bread. So the poor man, suffering, said, "If I have such bad luck, why am I trying to be a troubadour?"

La Gondola (The gondola)

[la gɔndola]

1 **Meco in barchetta celere**
meːkoin barketːta ʧeːlere
With-me in little-boat quick

2 **Scendi, leggiadra Clori.**
ʃɛndi ledːdʒadra kloːri
get-in, lovely Cloris.

3 **Vieni, cerchiamo ai zeffiri**
vjeːni ʧerkjamo ai dzefːfiri
Come, let-us-seek of-the zephyrs

4 **Conforto degli ardori**
konfɔrto deʎːʎi ardoːri
comfort from-the heat

5 **Che riscaldano il dì.**
ke riskaldano il di
that heats-up the day.

6 **Vieni, già l'onda tremola**
vjeːni dʒa llonda treːmola
Come, already the-wave shimmering

7 **È specchio della luna,**
ɛ sspɛkːkjo delːla luːna
is mirror of-the moon,

8 **E come l'aure baciano**
e kkoːme laure baːʧano
and just-as the-breezes kiss

9 **La placida laguna**
la plaːʧida laguːna
the peaceful lagoon

10 **Te bacieran così.**
te baʧeraːn kozi
you they-will-kiss thus.

11 **Vieni, e il tuo crin nerissimo**
vjeːnieil tuo kriːn neriːsːimo
Come, and the your hair very-black

12 **In preda all'aure ondeggi,**
in prɛːdalːlaureondɛdːdʒi
in prey to-the-breezes let-wave,

13 **E del mio core il palpito**
e del mio kɔːre il palpito
and of my heart the beating

14 **Coll'ondeggiar pareggi,**
kolːlondedːdʒaːr paredːdʒi
with-the-waving let-be-compared,

15 **Se pareggiar si può.**
se pparedːdʒaːr si pwɔ
if to-compare one can.

16 **Vedrai nel cielo limpido**
vedrai nel ʧeːlo limpido
You-will-see in-the heaven clear

17 **Brillar lucenti stelle,**
brilːlaːr luʧɛnti stelːle
shine glowing stars,

18 **A cui due luci fulgide**
a kkui due luːʧi fuldʒide
to which two lights shining

19 **Iddio creò sorelle,**
idːdio kreɔ sorɛlːle
God created sisters,

20 **E il tuo bel viso ornò.**
eil tuo bɛl viːzornɔ
and the your beautiful face adorned.

21 **Scendi, vezzosa Cloride,**
ʃɛndi vetːtsoːza kloːride
Step-down, lovely Cloris,

22 **E me vedrai beato,**
e mme vedrai beaːto
and me you-will-see blessed,

23 **E in estasi soavissima**
e in ɛstazi soaviːsːima
and in ecstasy very-gentle

24 **Di te seduto a lato**
di te seduːto alːlaːto
of you seated at side

25 **Mi pascerò d'amor.**
mi paʃːʃerɔ damoːr
myself I-shall-nourish with-love.

26 **E la tua destra candida**
e lla tua dɛstra kandida
And your right-hand white

27 **Al petto mollemente**
al pɛtːto molːlemɛnte
at-the bosom softly

28 **Fa che mi possa premere,**
fa kke mmi pɔsːsa prɛːmere
make that me may-be-able to-press,

29 **E il palpito frequente**
eil palpito frekwɛnte
and the beating frequent

30 **Intenda del mio cor.**
intɛnda del mio kɔːr
feel of my heart.

Poetic idea: "Come out with me for a boatride, and we will enjoy the cool breeze under the moonlight, my love."

This is another of Donizetti's reminiscences of Italy, written in the relatively cold climate of Paris. The gondola mentioned in the title typifies Venice, and the lagoon (line 9) is the calm water that surrounds Venice, shielded from the Adriatic Sea by the natural sea wall of the island called Lido.

The text has a male point of view, but this did not prevent Donizetti from composing the kind of a brilliant showpiece that is usually sung by a female voice. Audiences apparently enjoyed hearing a soprano give expression to a man's romantic fantasy. A modern soprano also need not miss out on the opportunity to enjoy this vocal challenge.

Source: *"La Gondola,"* first edition 1839). Copy at Milan. Original key:

Below the title appears the word usually a song that has a more popular c. a *romanza*.

La Gondola

Poet unknown

Gaetano Donizetti

Allegro con brio

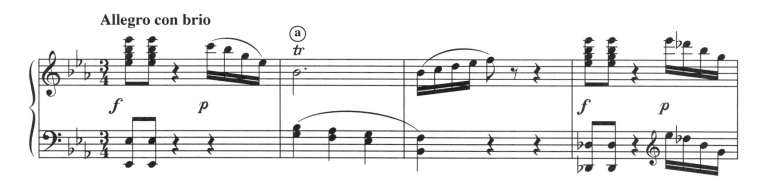

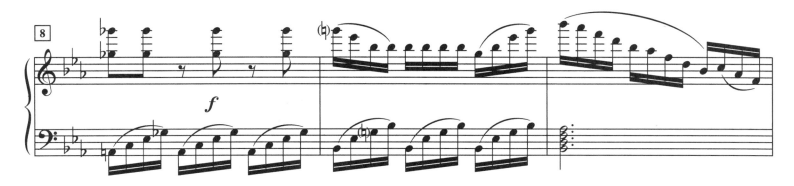

ⓐ All trills in this song are to be played or sung rapidly, beginning on the written note.

ⓑ All grace notes in this song are to be performed quickly and ahead of the beat, except in measure 57 (see note).

Literal translation: Climb into the quick little boat with me, lovely Cloris. Come, let us find breezes that will cool us from the heat of the day.

© Donizetti's slur stands for a *portamento* here. Slur the syllable *"-na"* upwards a half step. Do not sustain the upper tone, but sing it staccato. The staccato note should be sung as late as it is possible to do and still have time to breathe and re-enter on time in the next measure.

ⓓ The third sixteenth note requires an extra impulse of breath.

Come, already the shimmering waves reflect the moonlight and the breezes will kiss you just as they kiss the lagoon.

di, vie - ni!

Vie - ni, e il tu-o crin ne - ris-si - mo_____ in prɛ-da al-l'au-re on-dɛg - gi,

e_ del_ mi-o cɔ-re il pal-pi-to col-l'on-deg-giar_ pa - reg - gi,

rall. *a tempo*

colla parte *a tempo*

se pa - reg - giar si puɔ, se pa-reg-giar si_ puɔ. Viɛ -

cresc. *p*

(e) Sing both grace notes as appoggiaturas, that is, on the beat. The first appoggiatura is sung as an eighth note, the second as a sixteenth.

Come, loosen your black hair to wave in the breeze, and see if the beating of my heart is just as wild.

f̂ Sing a *portamento* as in measure 32.

In the clear sky you will see bright stars glowing; God made two sisters for them, the bright eyes that shine in your face.

(g) Begin the cadenza either on or after the second beat. Sing the cadenza freely, but in one breath. Lengthen any note of the cadenza as much as you wish.

Step in, Clori, and you will see me happy, in sweetest ecstasy;

seated by you, I will feast on love. And let your white hand softly press on my bosom

(h) If a full tremolo is not satisfactory, hold the highest and lowest chord tones and tremolo the inner ones.

(i) The source copy has no rest after the last two notes of measure 112. Donizetti may have intended to write a rest, as shown here. Or, he may have intended the last two notes to be sixteenths with a legato connection to the next measure.

(j) Follow the same instructions as for the cadenza in measure 77.

to feel the rapid beating of my heart.

L'amante spagnuolo

[lamˈante spaɲːˈnwɔlo]

korːri destrjɛr dɛ ʧɛːlere
1 **Corri destrier, deh, celere!**
Run, battle-horse, please, quickly!

korːri la via divoːra!
2 **Corri! La via divora!**
Run! The road eat-up!

rɛːkami akːkantoalːlanʤelo
3 **Recami accanto all'angelo**
Carry-me to-the-side of-the-angel

ke lla mia vitainfjoːra.
4 **Che la mia vita infiora.**
that — my life decks-with-flowers.

dɛ pria ke llalbain ʧɛːlo
5 **Deh, pria che l'alba in cielo**
Please, before that the-dawn in sky

spandail suo rɔːzeo veːlo,
6 **Spanda il suo roseo velo,**
stretches — its rosy veil

lavːvɛrtail tuo nitriːto
7 **L'avverta il tuo nitrito**
may-her-inform — your neighing

keil suo fedel tornɔ
8 **Che il suo fedel tornò.**
that — her faithful-one returned.

eil vɔlto a llɛi di ʤuːbilo
9 **E il volto a lei di giubilo**
And the face of her with joy

tu ʃʃintilːlar farai
10 **Tu scintillar farai,**
you to-sparkle will-cause,

e dde swɔi di deliːtsja
11 **E de' suoi dì delizia,**
and of her days delight,

o mio destrjɛr si sarai
12 **O mio destrier, sì, sarai.**
oh, my steed, yes, you-will-be.

verːra la man pudiːka
13 **Verrà la man pudica**
Will-come the hand modest

a kkaretːtsartiamiːka
14 **A carezzarti amica,**
to caress-you as-a-friend,

e mmen di te feliːʧe
15 **E men di te felice**
and less than you happy

io stesːso alːlor sarɔ
16 **Io stesso allor sarò.**
I myself then shall-be.

Poetic idea: "Run quickly, my steed, and carry me to my beloved."

Like "*La Gondola,*" this song takes a male point of view but can be sung by a brilliant singer of either sex. In the Romantic era, with its unprecedented adulation of female operatic stars, music lovers were perfectly willing to hear a coloratura soprano portray a dashing, impetuous horseman.

Tarantini was the poet of several of Donizetti's songs, including "*Viva il matrimonio,*" found later in this volume. He also wrote librettos for other composers, but not for Donizetti.

Source: *Soirées d'automne à l'Infrascata* (Autumn evenings at Infrascata) (Naples: B. Girard, 1837). Copy at Rome. Original key: G major. Voice part in soprano clef.

Under the title appears the word *bolero,* a typically Spanish dance in triple meter.

L'amante spagnuolo

Leopoldo Tarantini

Gaetano Donizetti

Allegretto

Cor - ri de - strier, deh, ce - le - re!___ Cor - ri,

cor - ri! La___ via di - vo - ra! Re - ca - mi___ ac-can-to al -

Literal translation: Run quickly, my steed, run! Eat up the road! Carry me to

the angel who makes my life beautiful. Before dawn spreads its rosy light in the sky, let her know by your neighing that her faithful lover has returned.

a) The source copy has only a crescendo over measure 29.

And you will make her face light up with joy, and you will be the delight of her life. Her chaste hand will give you a friendly caress, and I will be only a little less

64 ■ *L'amante spagnuolo*

happy than you!

Vincenzo Bellini, a marble statue by Ambrogio Borghi, dedicated in 1881 at La Scala Theater, Milan. From an Italian musical news magazine, Il Teatro illustrato, December 1881.

Lamento per la morte di Bellini
[lamento per la mɔrte di belːliːni]   (Lament for the death of Bellini)

venːne sulːlaːliai   dzɛfːfiri
1 **Venne sull'ali ai   zeffiri**
Came   on-the-wings of-the zephyrs

aʎːʎiːtaliun   sospiːro
2 **Agl'Itali un   sospiro:**
to-the-Italies a sigh:

ɛːra   delːlɔrfeo   siːkulo
3 **Era   dell'Orfeo   Siculo**
it-was of-the-Orpheus Sicilian

ultimoe ttriste spiːro
4 **Ultimo e triste   spiro;**
last and sad   breath;

ɛːra   ladːdio   del   fiʎːʎo
5 **Era   l'addio   del   figlio**
it-was the-goodbye of-the son

ke   mmwɔrein straːnjo swɔl
6 **Che   muore in   stranio   suol.**
that dies   on   foreign   soil.

komːmɔsːsaitaljal   nuntsjo
7 **Commossa, Italia al   nunzio**
Touched,   Italy to-the messenger

di kozi ria   zventuːra
8 **Di così ria   sventura**
of such guilty misfortune

pjandʒe   sul faːto barbaro
9 **Piange   sul fato barbaro,**
mourns   on fate cruel

kei   swɔi miʎːʎor le   fuːra
10 **Che i suoi miglior le   fura,**
that — its   best-ones from-it stole,

eil   pjanto   delːlitaːlja
11 **E   il   pianto   dell'Italia**
and the   weeping of-Italy

a llɛːkoin   straːnjo swɔl
12 **Ha l'eco   in stranio   suol.**
has the-echo in foreign soil.

oːra keal   kɔːro andʒeːliko
13 **Ora che al   coro angelico**
Now that to-the choir angelic

tiunistio   o spirtoelɛtːto
14 **Ti   unisti,   o spirto eletto,**
yourself you-unite, o spirit chosen,

spjeːgai konʧɛnti flɛːbili
15 **Spiega i concenti flebili,**
unfold the harmonies mournful,

il kanto delːlafːfɛtːto
16 **Il canto dell'affetto,**
the song of-affection

e   pper udirti   ʎːʎandʒeli
17 **E   per   udirti   gl'angeli**
and so-as to-hear-you the-angels

tɛrːran   sospeːzo il   voːl
18 **Terran   sospeso   il   vol.**
will-keep suspended the flight.

forsei   konʧɛntiarmɔːniʧi
19 **Forse i   concenti armonici**
Perhaps the chords   harmonious

keakːkɔrdi   in paradiːzo
20 **Che accordi   in Paradiso**
that you-tune-up in Paradise

verːran   sulːlaːle   ai dzɛfːfiri
21 **Verran   sull'ale   ai zeffiri**
will-come on-wings of zephyrs

a konfortarʧial   riːzo
22 **A confortarci al   riso,**
to comfort-us to   smile,

e   ffien   ladːdio   del   fiʎːʎo
23 **E   fien   l'addio   del   figlio**
and may-they-be the-farewell of-the son

ke al   ʧɛl si   mɔsːse a vvol
24 **Che al   ciel si   mosse a vol.**
that toward Heaven himself moved in flight.

Vincenzo Bellini died at the age of thirty-three on September 23, 1835, at Puteaux near Paris. Sick and alone, Bellini was staying in a villa owned by friends who were in Paris at the time. At his death he was attended only by a gardener and by a rather inept physician. An autopsy verified natural causes of death which might now be diagnosed as cancer, but rumors flew about possible poisoning.

Europe mourned. When the news reached Milan nine days later, one person who was thrown into depression by the news was the great mezzo-soprano Maria Malibran. She had seen Bellini a few months earlier in Paris and ardently hoped that he would compose an opera for her. Hearing the news, she broke down and, with a hand to her forehead, said, "I feel that I shall not be very long in following him." Her prophecy came true when she herself died exactly one year after Bellini, on September 23, 1836.

When Bellini died, Donizetti was in Naples, preparing for the greatest triumph of his career, the premiere of *Lucia di Lammermoor* at the Teatro San Carlo on September 26. In a letter that Weinstock quotes at length, Donizetti recalled occasions on which Bellini and he had worked on new operas at the same theaters in Genoa, Milan and Paris, "and each time our relationship became that much closer." He also wrote self-deprecatingly, "I am waiting for some good verses from the very distinguished Maffei, who will have a double cause for tears, the death of a friend and the combining of his verses with my music."

When *"Lamento"* was published, it carried a dedication to Maria Malibran.

Line 2: *gl'Itali,* the Italies, are named in the masculine plural because of the political divisions of the time. In line 7 the spirit of Italy is invoked as *Italia* and named in the feminine singular.

Line 3: *Orfeo Siculo:* Orpheus was a famous singer in Greek mythology, and Bellini is addressed as the Sicilian Orpheus because he was born in Catania, on the eastern coast of Sicily.

Line 5: *figlio,* son, refers to Bellini as a son of Italy.

Line 10: *fura,* robs, is an obsolete, poetic word. A lover of Italian poetry would be reminded of a famous phrase written in the 1300s by Petrarch, *"Morte fura prima i migliori…"* death steals first the best ones.

Line 14: addresses Bellini directly, calling him a spirit who is chosen by God.

Source: *"Lamento per la morte di Bellini"* (Milan: T. Ricordi, 1860). Copy at Milan, A-55-57-8. Original key: F minor. This copy does not mention the dedication to Malibran. According to UTET, there was an earlier, undated edition published by T. Cottrau, Naples.

Lamento per la morte di Bellini

Andrea Maffei

Gaetano Donizetti

Literal translation: On the wings of the wind a sad sigh reached Italy;

it was the last, sad breath of the great songster of Sicily. It was the farewell of the son who dies on foreign soil. Grieving,
Italia replies to the messenger that brought such terrible news, bewailing the cruel fate that steals her best sons from her,

(a) Sing the grace notes quickly and before the beat.

and Italy's mourning is echoed in foreign lands. Now that you have joined the angelic choir,
o chosen one, release your mournful harmonies, your song of love, and angels will pause

in their flight to hear you. Perhaps the harmonies that you tune

in Heaven will come on zephyr's wings to comfort us with a smile. Let them be the last farewell of the son who moved upward in flight.

(b) 1) This cadenza was written by Donizetti with Malibran's voice in mind. If you wish to sing this song but the cadenza does not suit your voice, you are free to sing fewer notes, omit the highest notes, sing arpeggios instead of scales, or make any other changes that are consistent with the spirit of the words.

2) The cadenza apparently contains 25 notes, an uneven number. This is a musically effective way to group them: Sing the first quarter note in the measure as if it were a 16th note and the first two notes of the cadenza as 32nds. Sing the remaining 23 notes of the cadenza and the succeeding quarter note as if they were six groups of four 32nd notes.

Leonora

1 **Partir** **conviene:** **Leonora, addio.**
partiːr konvjɛːne leonɔːradːdio
To-depart is-necessary: Leonora, farewell.

2 **Dolce idol mio, pianger perché?**
dolt͡ʃeiːdol mio pjand͡ʒer perke
Sweet idol mine, weep why?

3 **Dolor d'un giorno, dolor mendace!**
dolor dun d͡ʒorno doloːr mendaːt͡ʃe
Sorrow of-a day, sorrow false!

4 **Nulla è fugace più dell'amor.**
nulːla ɛ ffugat͡ʃe pju ddelːlamoːr
Nothing is fleeting more than-love.

5 **Farà ritorno la vela amata;**
fara ritorno la veːlamaːta
Will return the sail loved;

6 **Sol te cangiata ritroverà.**
sol te kand͡ʒaːta ritrovera
only you changed it-will-find.

7 **All'onde infide io m'abbandono.**
alːlondeinfiːde io mabːbandoːno
To-waves treacherous I myself-submit.

8 **Dell'ora il suono sul cor piombò.**
delːloːrail swɔːno sul kɔr pjombɔ
Of-the-hour the sound on-the heart fell.

9 **Deh! guarda il cielo, vaga donzella;**
dɛ gwarda il t͡ʃɛːlo vaːga dond͡zɛlːla
Please look-at the sky, lovely young-woman

10 **La fida stella mai non cangiò.**
la fiːda stelːla mai non kand͡ʒɔ
The faithful star ever not changed.

11 **Per noi rinnova la capinera**
per noi rinːnɔːva la kapineːra
For us renews the blackcap

12 **Di primavera la sua canzon.**
di primavɛːra la sua kantsoːn
of spring — its song.

13 **Il tempo crudo tutto distrugge,**
il tɛmpo kruːdo tutːto distrudːd͡ʒe
The time cruel all destroys,

14 **Ma tutto fugge per ritornar.**
ma ttutːto fudːd͡ʒe per ritornaːr
but everything flees so-as-to return.

Poetic idea: "I shall be out on the sea for a long time, but do not worry, Leonora. When I return we will love each other just as we do now."

Donizetti's style indication is *allegretto scherzoso,* moderately lively and playfully. This is a significant key to interpretation. This farewell is not tragic. When the sailor returns to Leonora, they will love each other again, even if nature and time have changed them somewhat.

Line 6: *sol te cangiata* has an implied meaning that is not expressly stated. The poet is thinking of faithfulness in love and answering an implied question from Leonora as to whether he will still love her when he returns from his voyage. He says that if she changes her mind while he is away, it will be only *(sol)* she who changes; his love will not change.

Line 11: *la capinera,* the blackcap, is a small European warbler, the male of which has a black head.

Source: *"Leonora"* (Milan?: Ricordi?, no date). Copy at Milano. Original key: D.

According to UTET, this song was first published posthumously in *Dernières glanes musicales* (Last musical gleanings) (Naples: B. Girard, no date) with the anonymous Italian text and a French text by M. Escudier.

The music of *"Leonora"* was also published with the text *"Addio, Brunetta, son già lontano"* in the Neapolitan journal *Il Sìbilo* (The Hiss), October 5, 1843. It was reproduced in *Donizetti Society Journal,* 1974, along with an amusing article by Jeremy Commons about how he rediscovered this obscure periodical.

The single page of music is headed *Canzonetta* and carries a dedication to Donizetti's "friend Raffaele d'Auria." The text has

only one stanza, which also deals with a sailor saying goodbye to his love. To make the song seem more complete, a repetition of measures 22–29 is indicated. The same key and style marking are used; a few rhythms are changed to accommodate the text. In addition to the *rall.* at measure 34, there is a *calando* at measure 37 and a fermata on the rest in measure 39. The fermata in measure 40 is marked *lungo,* and the final measure bears the word *smorzando,* probably meant to apply to the long note in measure 40.

Weinstock, New Grove and UTET all list *"Addio, Brunetta"* and *"Leonora"* as separate songs without noting that they are musically almost identical. It is not clear which version came first, but *"Leonora"* is published here because it is more complete and has a text that is wittier and more open to a variety of interpretations.

Leonora

Poet unknown

Gaetano Donizetti

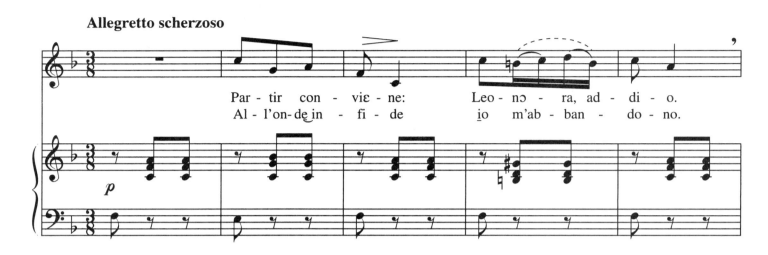

Allegretto scherzoso

Par - tir con - vie - ne: Leo - nɔ - ra, ad - di - o.
Al - l'on - de in - fi - de io m'ab - ban - do - no.

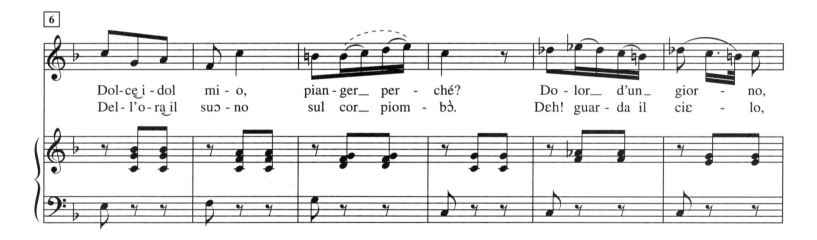

Dol - ce i - dol mi - o, pian - ger_ per - ché? Do - lor_ d'un_ gior - no,
Del - l'o - ra il suɔ - no sul cor_ piom - bɔ. Dɛh! guar - da il ciɛ - lo,

do - lor_ men - da - ce! Nul - la ɛ̀ fu - ga - ce più del - l'a - mor.
va - ga_ don - zɛl - la; la fi - da_ stel - la mɑi non_ can - giɔ.

Literal translation: 1) I must go; farewell, Leonora! Sweet idol of mine, why weep? One day's sorrow is a false sorrow!
Nothing is more fleeting than love.

2) I am entrusting myself to the treacherous sea; the hour of parting has sounded. Just look to the sky,
lovely maiden; the faithful stars never change.

Refrain: The sail you love to see will return; you will have changed (but not I!). Leonora, farewell!

3) For us the warbler will renew its springtime singing. Time destroys all, but only so that all return anew.

ma - ta; sol te can - gia - ta ri - tro - ve - rà,

sol te__ can - gia - ta ri - tro - ve - rà. Ad - dio, Leo -

no - ra, Leo - no - ra, ad - di -

- o, ad - di - o!

Le petit montagnard

[lə pəti mõ ta ɲar]

(The mountain lad)

u vrə mwa   bɔ nə   mɛ rə
1 Ouvre-moi,   bonne   mère,
Open-for-me, good   mother,

ʒe rə vjɛ̃ zo   pe i
2 Je reviens au   pays
I   return to-the birthplace

kõ sɔ le   ta   mi zɛ rə
3 Consoler   ta   misère.
to-console your destitution.

sɛ   ʒy ljɛ̃ sɛ   tõ   fis
4 C'est Julien, c'est ton   fils.
It-is Julian, it-is your son.

kã   ʒe   fɥi ta   də mœ rə
5 Quand j'ai   fui ta   demeure,
When I-have left your dwelling,

ty   ma   di tã   plœ rã
6 Tu   m'as   dit en   pleurant,
you to-me-have said with crying,

fo dra til   kə   ʒə mœ rə
7 "Faudra-t-il   que   je meure
"Is-it-necessary that I   die

sã   rə vwar mõ   nã fã
8 Sans   revoir mon enfant?"
without seeing my   child?"

na ty   pɑ   su və nã sə
9 N'as-tu   pas souvenance
Of-it-have-you not memory

də sə   ʒwa jø   rə frɛ̃
10 De ce   joyeux   refrain
of this   happy   refrain

kə   ʒe   rə di   tã frã sə
11 Que j'ai   redit   en France
that I-have repeated in France

pur tə ga ɲe   dy pɛ̃
12 Pour te   gagner du pain?
for you to-earn some bread?

e ku tə bɔ nə mɛ rə
13 Écoute, bonne mère,
Listen, good   mother,

œ   brɥi ply   du   zã kɔr
14 Un bruit plus doux encor,
a   sound more sweet yet,

e ku tã   ta   ʃo mjɛ rə
15 Écoute en ta   chaumière
hear in   your cottage

sɔ ne   mɛ trwa lwi dɔr
16 Sonner mes trois louis d'or
sound my   three louis of-gold.

lã fã   də la   mõ ta ɲə
17 L'enfant de la   montagne
The-child of the mountain

ɛ̃ si   ʃã tɛ   la nɥi
18 Ainsi chantait la nuit
thus   sang   at night

kã   lə   ʃɛ̃   la kõ pa ɲə
19 Quand le   chien l'accompagne
when the dog   him-accompanies

lwɛ̃ dy   po vrə re dɥi
20 Loin du   pauvre réduit.
far   from-the poor   poor-lodging.

su   la ne ʒə ki   tõ bə
21 Sous la neige qui   tombe
Under the snow that falls

dɔr lɔb ʒɛ   də sɛ   vø
22 Dort l'objet   de ses vœux.
sleeps the-object of his vows.

e lɑs la   mɛ mə tõ bə
23 Hélas, la   même tombe
Alas, the same   tomb

le   re y ni tu   dø
24 Les réunit   tous deux.
them reunites all   two [both].

y nə mɔ dɛ stə pjɛ rə
25 Une   modeste pierre
A   modest   stone

di o   pa sã   syr pri
26 Dit au   passant   surpris,
says to-the passer-by surprised,

plœ re la po vrə mɛ rə
27 "Pleurez la pauvre mère,
"Mourn   the poor   mother,

plœ re lə tã drə fis
28 Pleurez le tendre fils."
mourn   the loving son."

Poetic idea: A poor lad, who has left home to earn money for his widowed mother, returns home at night and asks to be let in. The family's faithful dog leads him to his mother's grave. Now a gravestone tells us that both mother and son lie there.

Line 16: *louis d'or,* gold louis, was not a coin of Donizetti's time; mention of it places the poem in a nostalgic past. It represents a large amount of money to a peasant family. A gold louis in 1789 had a purchasing power equal to $50 or more today.

In this mature song interpretation marks abound; almost every phrase has specific marks of articulation or dynamics. Staccato marks in the first two stanzas emphasize the boy's youth and happy expectations; there are none in the third stanza. At measure 31 *pressez* (accelerate) is added to the crescendo; the tempo stops with the fermata in measure 43, and measure 45 is again at the first tempo. Probably the same acceleration should occur at measure 71. The third stanza has a slower tempo.

Source: *"Le petit montagnard,"* in a series entitled *L'Aurore* (Mainz: B. Schotts Söhne, no date, Edition no. 7163). Copy at Cambridge, Mass. Original key: A minor. Texts in French and German *("Der kleine Alpenknabe")*.

Poet: "Mme. ___."

According to UTET, the manuscript of this song bears a dedication to Mme. Zélie de Coussy, who also received the dedication of the opera *Don Pasquale* and of the song *"Tu mi chiedi si t'adoro,"* found in this volume. She and her husband, who was Donizetti's Paris banker, were among his closest friends. *"Le petit montagnard"* was published in *Fiori di sepolcro* (Flowers of the sepulchre), therefore posthumously. The Schott publication is not a first edition.

Le petit montagnard

Poet unknown

Gaetano Donizetti

Literal translation: "Open the door, dear mother. I'm coming back home to relieve your suffering.

(a) All grace notes in this song are to be performed quickly and before the beat.

It's Julien, your son. When I left home, you said tearfully, 'Must I die without seeing my child?' Open up, dear mother.

N'as-tu pas sou-ve - nan - - - ce de ce joy-eux re - frain

que j'ai re-dit en Fran - - ce pour te ga-gner du pain, pour te ga-gner du

pain? É-cou-te, bon-ne mè - - re, un bruit plus doux en-

cor, é-cou-te en ta chau-miè - - re son-ner mes trois louis

2) "Don't you remember the jolly song that I sang all over France to earn some bread for you? Listen, dear mother, here's a sweeter sound yet; listen to my gold coins jingling!"

3) The mountain lad sang that way through the night until the dog led him far away from the poor cottage. Under the falling snow sleeps the one to whom he made his vows.

(b) The final three measures should be sung with the freedom of a cadenza. Take extra time for the breath in measure 111, dwell on the high note in measure 112, linger over the turn, and hold the final note for as long as your breath allows. The pianist times the chords to the mood and comfort of the singer. The final chord is released as the singer pronounces the *s* of *fils*.

Alas, the same tomb is the place where mother and son meet again. A modest stone says to the surprised passer-by: "Mourn for the poor mother, mourn for the poor son."

Les yeux noirs et les yeux bleus
[lɛ zjø nwa re lɛ zjø blø]

(Dark eyes and blue eyes)

1
a	kɛ	lɑ̃ ba ra	ɛ kstrɛ mə
Ah!	**quel**	**embarras**	**extrême!**
Ah,	what	uncertainty	extreme!

2
kɛl	tur mɑ̃	vjɛ̃	mə sɛ zir
Quel	**tourment**	**vient**	**me saisir!**
What	torment	comes	me to-overcome!

3
ɑ̃ trə	dø	bo te	kə	ʒɛ mə
Entre	**deux**	**beautés**	**que**	**j'aime**
Between	two	beauties	that	I-love

4
dɛ	də mɛ̃	il	fo	ʃwa zir
Dès	**demain**	**il**	**faut**	**choisir.**
by	tomorrow	it	is-necessary	to-choose.

5
ly	nɛ	blɔ̃ də	lo	trə	bry nə
L'une	**est**	**blonde,**	**l'autre**	**est**	**brune,**
The-one	is	blond,	the-other	is	brunette,

6
dɛ	dø	ko te	mɔ̃	kœ	rɛ	pri
Dès	**deux**	**côtés**	**mon**	**coeur**	**est**	**pris;**
from	two	sides	my	heart	is	taken.

7
ɑ̃	na bɑ̃ dɔ ne	ry nə
En	**abandonner**	**une,**
Of-them	to-abandon	one,

8
nɔ̃	ʒa mɛ	ʒə nə	lə	pɥi
Non	**jamais!**	**je ne**	**le**	**puis!**
no,	never!	I not	it	can-do!

9
də	kla ra la	vwa	du	se	tɑ̃ drə
De	**Clara la**	**voix**	**douce**	**et**	**tendre**
Of	Clara the	voice	sweet	and	tender

10
sɑ̃	rə tu	ra	sy	mə	ʃar me
Sans	**retour**	**a**	**su**	**me**	**charmer;**
without	return	has	known-how	me	to-charm.

11
ze li a	pø tɔ̃	sə	de fɑ̃ drə
Zélia,	**peut-on**	**se**	**défendre**
Zelia,	can-one	himself	forbid

12
pur	tu ʒur	də	ta dɔ re
Pour	**toujours**	**de**	**t'adorer?**
for	always	—	you-to-adore?

13
dɑ̃	la zyr	də	tɛ	zjø	ʒe	py	li rə
Dans	**l'azur**	**de**	**tes**	**yeux**	**j'ai**	**pu**	**lire,**
In	the-blue	of	your	eyes	I-have	been-able	to-read,

14
ma	kla ra	du	zɛ spwar	də	bɔ nœr
Ma	**Clara,**	**doux**	**espoir**	**de**	**bonheur.**
my	Clara,	sweet	hope	of	happiness.

15
ze li a	tɛ	zjø	nwar	tɔ̃	su ri rə
Zélia,	**tes**	**yeux**	**noirs,**	**ton**	**sourire,**
Zelia,	your	eyes	black,	your	smile,

16
mɔ̃	prɔ mi	zœ̃	dɛ stɛ̃	ɑ̃ ʃɑ̃ tœr
M'ont	**promis**	**un**	**destin**	**enchanteur.**
me-have	promised	a	destiny	enchanting.

Poetic idea: "I am crazy about two women. I am supposed to choose between them by tomorrow, but how can I?"

This song is nothing other than a French adaptation of Donizetti's Italian song, "*Occhio nero incendiator*" found on page 115 of this book. In supplying French words to a pre-existing song, Monnier gave names to the two competing loves. As a result the French song has a stronger sense of being sung from a male point of view.

The song collection that contained "*Occhio nero incendiator*" must have been published in 1833 or before, and the French version was published after 1835.

Source: (1) *"Les yeux noirs et les yeux bleus"* (Paris: Bernard Latte, no date). Copy at Paris, D. 3510 (6). Original key: E major.

UTET lists this song and the Italian version as different songs; in fact, they are musically identical except for insignificant changes in note values to accommodate the texts.

LES YEUX NOIRS ET LES YEUX BLEUS

ROMANCE

Lith Guillet

PAROLES D'ÉTIENNE MONNIER

MUSIQUE DE

G. DONIZETTI 2.f 50.c

Paris, chez **BERNARD LATTE** Éditeur, Boulevart des Italiens, N.° 2

This cover art from the Paris edition shows a casually dressed gentleman in elegant
surroundings, holding miniature portraits of the two women whom he must choose between.
A comical figurine near his left hand seems out of keeping with the other decor.

Les yeux noirs et les yeux bleus

Étienne Monnier

Gaetano Donizetti

ⓐ Sing the grace note quickly and before the beat.

Literal translation: 1) Ah, what a problem! What torment I'm going through! I love two beautiful women, and I have to choose between them by tomorrow! One is blond, the other

dark, and both have taken my heart. Abandon one of them? No, never! I cannot do it.
2) Clara's sweet and tender voice has charmed me. Could a person refrain from adoring Zelia forever?

3) In the blue of your eyes, my Clara, I can read a sweet hope of happiness. Zelia, your dark eyes, your

smile, have promised me an enchanting destiny.

L'ora del ritrovo

(The hour of meeting)

[lo:ra del ritrɔ:vo]

o:dieli:za   kwestaɛ lo:ra
1 Odi,   Elisa: questa è l'ora,
Listen, Elisa: this   is the-hour

kai   prefis:sal   mio veni:r
2 Ch'hai   prefissa   al mio venir.
that-you-have pre-arranged for my   coming.

per ʎiamantioɲ:ɲi   dimɔ:ra
3 Per gli   amanti ogni   dimora
For   the   lovers every   waiting

ɛ ttormɛnto da mmori:r
4 È tormento   da   morir.
is torment   for to-die.

ɔ   pprega:to la̯er   fosko
5 Ho   pregato   l'aer   fosco
I-have begged   the-air dark

ke   ssaf:fret:ti per pjeta̯
6 Che   s'affretti   per   pietà,
that it-hasten   for pity;

ma   pprome̯s:so̯il   vitʃin   bɔsko
7 M'ha   promesso il   vicin   bosco
to-me-has promised   the nearby   woods

ke̯il   segre:to serbeɾa̯
8 Che il   segreto   serberà.
that the secret   it-will-keep.

fwɔr ke̯il   palpito del   kɔ:re
9 Fuor che il   palpito del   core
Aside from the beating of-the heart

tut:to̯al   kɔr   ripozeɾa̯
10 Tutto   al   cor   riposerà.
everything of-the heart will-rest.

il   segre:to del:lamo:re
11 Il   segreto   dell'amore
The   secret   of-love

so:lo̯amɔr konoʃ:ʃeɾa vjɛ:ni
12 Solo amor conoscerà. Vieni!
only love   will-know. Come!

Poetic idea: "Please come with me, beloved; you promised! It is not dark yet, but we can be alone among the nearby trees."

In 1842 Donizetti was in Vienna to conduct the premiere of *Linda di Chamounix* with the title role sung by Eugenia Tadolini (born 1809). The opera had a great success, and Donizetti was highly pleased with the leading lady. Like *Lucia di Lammermoor,* written in 1835, *Linda* also has a mad scene, and Donizetti wrote that as Tadolini performed it *Linda's* mad scene was "on a higher plane. . . than any of the other scenes I have written for madwomen."

On May 24, 1842, following the third performance of *Linda,* Donizetti wrote in a letter that he had just completed "a little musical album (to pay for the trip)." This was published as *Inspirations viennoises* (Viennese inspirations). The collection includes five *ariette,* of which this song is the third, and two *duettini,* all on texts by Carlo Guaita.

Donizetti complimented Tadolini by dedicating this song to her, and he must have had her voice in mind, as he was working with her daily during this period. She had great success in comic roles, and this song employs her facility for rapid diction. As is true of other songs in this book, the male viewpoint of the poem was no hindrance to performance by a soprano.

Tadolini sang various roles for Donizetti in Naples and Paris. She was an early advocate of Verdi and sang the premiere of Verdi's *Alzira,* but he rejected her for *Macbeth,* saying, "Tadolini's voice has something of the angelic, and I would like Lady Macbeth's voice to have something of the diabolic."

Source: *Ispirazioni viennesi* (Milan: T. Ricordi, no date). Copy at Milan, A-55-57-11/A. Original key: A major.

According to UTET, the first edition was published in Naples by B. Girard, no date given.

L'ora del ritrovo

Carlo Guaita

Gaetano Donizetti

Literal translation: Hear me, Elisa: this is the time when you said that I may

come. For a lover every moment of waiting is a deadly torment.

I have asked the darkness to come quickly, please, and the nearby woods have promised to keep our secrets.

Aside from our beating hearts, everything will be quiet. The secret of our love, only love itself will know.

(a) Linger over the notes of the turn.

Non amerò che te!

(I love only you)

a   se   ddamoːre un palpito
1 **Ah! se d'amore   un palpito**
Ah, if of-love   a   palpitation

sentiːr tu   vwɔi per me
2 **Sentir tu   vuoi per me,**
to-feel you want for me,

in tɛrːra ein   tʃɛl koʎːʎiandʒeli
3 **In terra e in ciel   cogli   angeli**
on earth and in Heaven with-the angels

non amerɔ   ke   tte
4 **Non amerò   che te.**
none I-shall-love but you.

per te fantʃulːla e   pɔːvera
5 **Per te, fanciulla   e   povera,**
For you, young-girl and poor,

il   mondo io laʃːʃerɔ
6 **Il   mondo io lascierò,**
the world I   shall-leave;

nelːlamoːr tuo   la   patria
7 **Nell'amor tuo   la   patria**
in-love   your the homeland

tutːtoin te   soːla avrɔ
8 **Tutto in te   sola   avrò.**
all   in you alone I-shall-have.

ne   ddir mudrai   vjɛn   meːko
9 **Né   dir m'udrai,   "Vien   meco,**
Nor say me-you-will-hear: "Come with-me,

fantʃulːla un rikːkoio   son
10 **Fanciulla, un ricco   io son."**
girl,   a   rich-man I am."

non troveranːnoun ɛːko
11 **Non troveranno un eco**
Not would-find an echo

nelːlalma tua tai swɔn
12 **Nell'alma tua tai suon.**
in-the-soul your such sounds.

puːra dafːfɛtːtiumaːni
13 **Pura d'affetti   umani,**
Pure for-emotions human,

bɛlːla   del tuo   kandoːr
14 **Bella   del tuo   candor,**
beautiful for your honesty,

ne llaɾi   twɔi rimaːni
15 **Né lari   tuoi rimani;**
nor ancestors your you-remain;

sol io vivrɔ   damoːr
16 **Sol io vivrò   d'amor!**
only I shall-live from-love!

ke   sse lavermi   alːlaːto
17 **Che se l'avermi   allato**
For if having-me at-your-side

ti spjaːtʃe   io partirɔ
18 **Ti spiace...   io partirò;**
you displeases, I   shall-leave;

sol oːve   a   tte sia   graːto
19 **Sol ove   a   te sia   grato**
only where to you may-be pleasing

a   tte ritorneɾɔ
20 **A te   ritornerò.**
to you I-shall-return.

e   sse kandʒar di tɛmpre
21 **E   se cangiar di tempre**
And if changing of feelings

il   tʃɛːloun   di   vorːra
22 **Il   cielo   un dì   vorrà,**
the Heaven one day shall-will,

il   noːme mio per sɛmpre
23 **Il   nome mio per sempre**
the name my for always

il   noːme tuo   saɾa
24 **Il   nome tuo   sarà.**
the name yours will-be.

Poetic idea: "I will love only you, even though for now you are not willing to come away with me and be my love."

Donizetti saw the possibilities of youthful, impetuous passion in this poem. His choice of an extremely fast tempo makes this an energetic and persuasive song.

Line 4: *Non... che* in Italian means "only." The French language has a similar grammatical construction with *"ne... que."*

Lines 6: *Il mondo io lascierò* implies that the lover would have to give up his social station, perhaps even his nationality, to marry the girl.

Lines 11–12: *Non... suon* expresses the lover's realization that this girl would not be impressed by wealth, probably because of her moral qualities mentioned in the next lines. The quiet monotone of measures 63–65 imitates the furtiveness of a deceitful man who pretends to be wealthy in order to seduce a girl; the lover implies that he is not that kind of person and that she would not be impressed if he were.

Line 15: *Lari* were household idols representing

ancestral spirits, believed by the ancient Romans to protect their homes. They are mentioned here as a metaphor for the girl's family home. *Né* as a conjunction always has a negative connotation; it would be inappropriate here. In this line *né* stands for *nei,* "in the."

Line 16: *Sol... d'amor* means that the lover will have only his longing, never any satisfaction.

The song is dedicated to Madame de Coussy, who also received the dedications to *"Le petit montagnard"* and *"Tu mi chiedi si t'adoro."*

Source: *"Non amerò che te"* (Milan: G. Ricordi, no date, catalog 13590). Copy at Milan, A-55.57.27. Also at Rome, B.173.16. Original key: C major.

The two source copies are identical except that the copy in Rome has a line stating *"Versione dal francese di G. Vitali."* This indicates that this song once existed in French and that it was translated into Italian by G. Vitali. I have not found a French version, nor is it listed by UTET; possibly it never existed and the reference to it was a mistake.

Non amerò che te

Poet unknown

Gaetano Donizetti

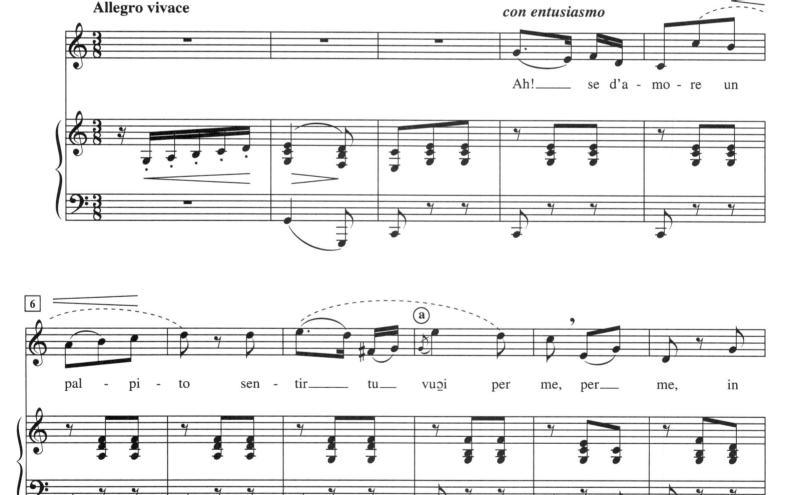

(a) Perform the grace note before the beat and quickly. The upward slur is sung on the vowel [ɔ].

Literal translation: If you feel a little love for me,

I will love no one but you either on earth or in Heaven with the angels. For you, a poor girl, I will leave the world; your love

will be all the homeland I will have.

But you will not hear me say, "Come to me, girl, I am rich."

Words like that would not find any echo in your heart. Pure in your human feelings, beautiful in your innocence,

you are staying in your ancestral home. I will live only for my love!

If having me near you

displeases you, I will go. I would only be in a place where it pleases you. And if someday Heaven wills that you change

your heart, then my name will become your name forever.

Occhio nero incendiator

ɔk:kjo nerointʃendjator
1 **Occhio nero incendiator,**
Eye, dark, incendiary,

io non sɔ se un bɛn sɛi tu
2 **Io non so se un ben sei tu.**
I not know if a good are you.

lɔk:kjoad:dzur:roɛ ddoltʃe pju
3 **L'occhio azzurro è dolce più,**
The-eye blue is sweet more,

pjɛn dun tɛnero laŋgwor
4 **Pien d'un tenero languor.**
full of-a tender languishing.

gwɛr:ral kɔr lɔk:kjo nero mi fa
5 **Guerra al cor l'occhio nero mi fa,**
War to-the heart the-eye dark me makes,

patʃe e kalma lad:dzur:ro mi da
6 **Pace e calma l'azzurro mi dà.**
peace and calm the-blue me gives.

lɔk:kjo nero ɛ kkwel siɲ:ɲor
7 **L'occhio nero é quel signor,**
The-eye dark is such master;

moltoezidʒe e pp ɔko da
8 **Molto esige e poco dà.**
much it-demands and little gives.

ɛ tter:ribil nel:lo zdeɲ:ɲo
9 **È terribil nello sdegno,**
It-is terrible in scorn

pas:sad:dʒer nel:la pjeta
10 **Passaggier nella pietà.**
temporary in pity.

lɔk:kjoad:dzur:ro ɛaskozo ardor
11 **L'occhio azzurro é ascoso ardor,**
The-eye blue is hidden ardor,

pɔkostɛnta e mmolto fa
12 **Poco ostenta e molto fa,**
little it-displays and much does.

e kkompɛnsa un luŋgo amor
13 **E compensa un lungo amor**
and it-rewards a long love

kon segreta fedelta
14 **Con segreta fedeltà.**
with secret faithfulness.

ma llamore lla belta
15 **Ma l'amore e la beltà**
But love and — beauty

non dipɛnde del kolor
16 **Non dipende del color.**
not depend on color.

la mia dɛa bɛl:lɔk:kjo avra
17 **La mia Dea bell'occhio avrà**
The my goddess beautiful-eye will-have

se rrispɔnde lɔk:kjo al kɔr
18 **Se risponde l'occhio al cor.**
if responds the-eye to-the heart.

purke fred:do fal:latʃe non ɛ
19 **Purché freddo o fallace non è,**
Provided-that cold or deceptive not it-is,

nero ad:dzur:roɛun bɛl:lɔk:kjo per me
20 **Nero o azzurro è un bell'occhio per me.**
dark or blue is a beautiful-eye for me.

Poetic idea: "I'm attracted to two kinds of women, dark and fair, and they seem to have different personalities. But it won't matter in the end, because the one that loves me in return is going to be the most beautiful to me."

Whether the song is serious or teasing is a decision for the interpreter to make. Donizetti may have tipped the scale toward a playful interpretation by writing his music as a theme and variations. The simple chordal accompaniment remains the same for all four stanzas, while the voice explores many possibilities for ornamentation and rhythmic variations.

Line 1: *"Occhio nero"* is singular, as translated on this page, but has to be translated into English with the plural "eyes," as in the literal translation on the following pages. Also, the word *nero,* black, describes eyes that in English would be called dark brown.

This song appears in a collection that was published in 1833 or earlier, judging by a dedication to the reigning monarch. *"Les yeux noirs et les yeux bleus,"* also found in this book, is a French adaptation of this song. Both versions are included here because they produce such different aesthetic effects.

Source: This is the second song in *Raccolta di canzonette e duettini* (Milano: F. Lucca, no date). Copy at Milano, A-55.57.29. Original key: E major.

In *Raccolta* the whole song fills only two pages. Four separate staves carry four versions of the voice part vertically aligned over the accompaniment, which is printed only once.

Occhio nero incendiator

Poet unknown

Gaetano Donizetti

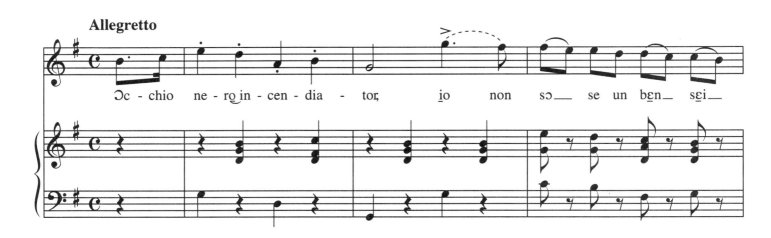

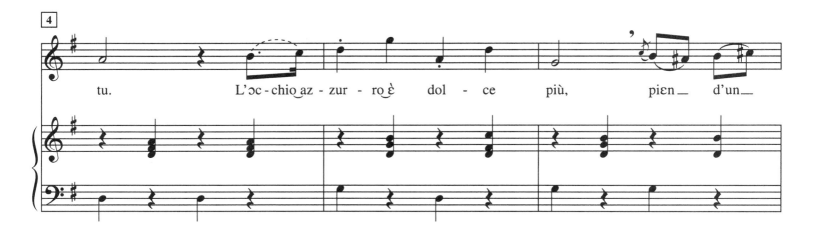

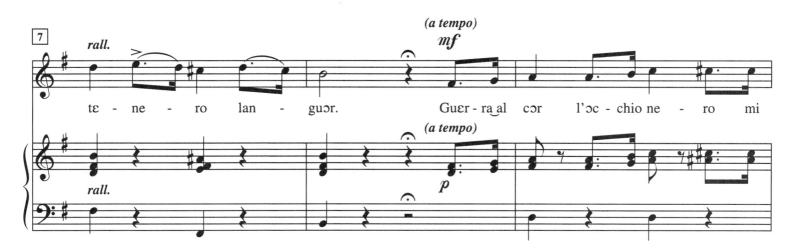

Literal translation: 1) Fiery, dark eyes, I don't know whether you are good for me; blue eyes are sweeter and filled with more tender longing. Dark eyes make war on my heart,

while blue ones make me feel peaceful and calm. 2) Dark eyes are dominating; they ask for a lot and give little. They are dreadful in their scorn, and only temporary in their pity.

tà. Guer - ra al cor l'oc - chio ne - ro mi fa, pa - ce e
cal - ma l'az - zur - ro mi dà, pa - ce e cal - ma l'az - zur - ro mi
dà. L'oc - chio az - zur - ro è a - sco - so ar - dor, po - co o -
sten - ta e mol - to____ fa, e com - pen - sa un lun - go a -

3) Blue eyes mean hidden passions; they show little but prove themselves in actions. They repay a long-time

118 ■ *Occhio nero incendiator*

love with secret fidelity. 4) But love and beauty do not

depend on color. My goddess's eyes will be beautiful to me if they are just responsive to my heart.

Se a te d'intorno scherza

(If a breeze around you plays)

se a tte dintorno skertsa
1 Se a te d'intorno scherza
If to you around plays

un nwɔːvo ddzefːfiretːto
2 Un nuovo zeffiretto,
a new little-breeze,

non rɛsti o dio neglɛtːto
3 Non resti, oh Dio, negletto!
not may-it-remain, oh God, neglected!

lakːkɔʎːʎi ɛun mio sospir
4 L'accogli: è un mio sospir.
Accept-it; it-is a my sigh.

kwel dzefːfiro respiːra
5 Quel zeffiro respira
That breeze breathes

fiŋ ke ti ddʒuŋgal kɔːre
6 Fin che ti giunga al core;
Until that you it-reaches at-the heart;

ɛ un mesːsadːdʒer damoːre
7 È un messagger d'amore,
it-is a messenger of-love,

di ddʒɔːja e di martir
8 Di gioia, e di martir.
of joy, and of martyrdom.

Poetic idea: "Please accept the message of longing and love that I am sending to you."

Donizetti often chose texts that lend themselves to role-playing: the gondolier, the lad from the mountains, the gypsy girl. In contrast, this poem carries a message for anyone at all who is in love.

Beginning with an inverted altered chord, the introduction has a rhythmic lightness that suits the image of the gentle breeze that is mentioned in the poem. The vocal melody rises impetuously at first and maintains a high tessitura throughout the song, employing each of the chromatic tones from the dominant up to the tonic. The first half of the poem is sung to a melody eight measures long while the accompaniment modulates through minor keys; a bit of text repetition allows the melody to be extended to a cadence in measure 13 on the dominant of the relative minor. After another modulatory phrase four measures long, the first melody briefly returns (measure 17, beat 4) in a varied form. In measure 21 the melody cadences and a coda begins that forms more than a third of the whole song. The last two lines of the poem are sung again and again with a variety of emotional inflections. As brief as it is, the song presents a model of Donizetti's skill in spinning a legato melody, one that unfolds naturally and avoids simple repetition.

Sources: (1) Autograph manuscript, The Pierpont Morgan Library, New York City. Original key: F major. Voice part in soprano clef. Key: F.

The single leaf of paper is printed with musical staves on both sides. The song is headed *"Romanza"* and signed *"Donizetti."*

(2) *"Se a te d'intorno scherza,"* published in the Neapolitan journal *Il Sìbilo* (The Hiss), April 4, 1844. It was reproduced in *Donizetti Society Journal,* 1974, along with an amusing article by Jeremy Commons about how he rediscovered this obscure periodical. He comments that its pages were small and that the print quality was not as clear as one would wish.

The single page of music is headed with the words *Romanza* and "from the album of Countess Angela Carradori." It was a common practice for musicians to respond to hospitality by copying a brief piece of music into the hostess's guest book. Just over the music are the words "Property of the publisher Giuseppe Fabricatore." Donizetti spent the first six months of 1844 in Vienna, so it must have been Fabricatore who sold the song to *Il Sìbilo.*

Since neither source was prepared for publication by Donizetti, the discrepancies between (1) and (2) cannot be finally resolved. The performer may choose between possibilities listed here.

Measure 4: (2) has a *diminuendo* rather than a *crescendo.*

Measure 11: (2) lacks the *accelerando.*

Measure 12, voice part: (1) has an ornament that is clearly written but is probably an error, nevertheless. The double-grace notes are the pitches F and E (in the original key of F), producing a lower neighbor figure that would be abnormal in the period. The alternative pitches D and E given in (2) are much more normal, and just as expressive. Notice that the stressed vowel [i] must be sung on the grace notes and sustained on the dotted quarter; the secondary vowel [o] occurs quickly at the end of the dotted quarter.

Measure 12, piano part: The somewhat unexpected notes on the first two beats are, however, quite clearly readable in both sources. Source (2) has a block chord in the piano on beat 3, followed by rests over which is a wide fermata. Source (1) has the broken chord figure shown in this edition with a wide fermata sign, just as he wrote it; the curved line embraces at least three notes, and the dot is between beats 3 and 4. This sign, which was also used by Schubert, shows that several notes are slowed down to accommodate the held tone in the voice. Fortunately, recent advances in music engraving allow us to re-introduce this useful symbol.

Measure 17, beat 4, piano part: (2) has a quarter rest in both hands.

Measure 21: (2) lacks the dynamic marking, as do measures 22, 23, 26 and 27.

Measure 24, piano part: On beat 1 source (2) has D in the left hand; source (1) has a note that can be read as either C or D. C is clearly preferable on stylistic grounds. On beat 4 the unexpected chord is given here as in (2); source (1) is unreadable at this point because of erasures and corrections.

Measure 32, piano part: (2) lacks the seventh of the chord on beat 3.

Se a te d'intorno scherza

Poet unknown

Gaetano Donizetti

Se a te d'in-tor-no

scher - za un nuɔ - vo zef - fi - ret - to, non

rɛ - sti, oh Dịo, ne - glɛt - to! L'ac - cɔ - gli: ɛ un mịo so -

Literal translation: If you feel a new breeze playing around you, do not let it be ignored. Accept it: it is a

sigh from me. That breeze keeps wafting until it reaches your heart. It is a messenger of love, of joy and of my suffering.

Sull'onda cheta e bruna (Over the silent wa.

Barcarola

sul:londa   ke:ta e   bbru:na
1 **Sull'onda   cheta e   bruna,**
On-the-wave   silent and   dark,

pria   ke   sorga   la   lu:na
2 **Pria   che   sorga   la   luna,**
before   that   may-rise   the   moon,

velo:tʃeo   gondoljɛr
3 **Veloce, o   gondolier,**
quickly, o   gondolier,

dɛ   solkail   tuo   sentjɛr
4 **Deh,   solca   il tuo   sentier,**
please,   embark-on — your   path,

ma ve   ke   la tua   pro:ra
5 **Ma veh   che   la tua   prora,**
but see   that — your   prow

karɛt:tsi   ljɛ:vɛil   mar
6 **Carezzi   lieve   il   mar.**
may-caress   lightly   the   sea.

a   so:lo   sol   leono:ra
7 **A   solo   sol   Leonora,**
at   only   only   Leonora,

ke   kantansjo:za   oɲ:ɲo:ra
8 **Che   canta ansiosa   ogn'ora,**
who   sings   anxiously   all-the-while,

o:da   del   kɔr   tral   palpitar
9 **Oda   del   cor   tra'l   palpitar**
may-hear   of-the   heart   with-the   beating

del   fi:doama:nte   il   remigar
10 **Del   fido   amante   il   remigar.**
of-the   faithful   lover   the   rowing.

Poetic idea: "Gondolier, row so quietly that my beloved will be able to hear the beating of my heart."

The scene is in Venice, the city of canals, before moonrise on a dark evening. A *barcarola* is a song in 6/8 meter associated with Venetian gondoliers. The word derives from a Venetian dialect word *barcaròl,* a professional boatman.

Nothing is known about the writing of this song nor why it remained unpublished. The manuscript was owned by the Cottrau family, descendants of Guillaume (or Guglielmo) Cottrau, a French composer who built up a music publishing business in Naples. Another member of the family, Teodoro Cottrau, composed the popular song, *"Santa Lucia."* The Cottrau firm issued many of Donizetti's works. It is all the more puzzling that they did not publish this charming song.

Source: Autograph manuscript, Rome, Ms. 586. Original key: E-flat major. Voice part in bass clef.

The manuscript is a single sheet of paper, about 20 cm. high and 25 cm. wide, printed with 20 (!) musical staves. The tiny writing is in brown ink. Heading: *"Barcarola."* Other hands than Donizetti's have added three comments in Italian: at the upper right corner "Gift of Giulio Cottrau;" at the lower right "Autograph of Donizetti;" and on the reverse side "This autograph of Donizetti was acquired in 1884 from Giulio Cottrau."

Each musical system consists of five staves:

(1) contains the voice part in bass clef;

(2), which is also provided with a bass clef and key and meter signatures, remains empty until measure 21 where another voice enters, singing *"Zitto"* (Quiet!) and later adds some other comments, for which the text is illegible;

(3) remains empty except where it is used for some corrections to the voice part;

(4) and (5) contain the piano accompaniment.

UTET does not list this song. Weinstock lists it as an unpublished composition for two voices. The presence of the second voice suggests that this song may have been intended for inclusion in an opera, but in searching available scores I have not found it. Only New Grove lists a publication in Milan in 1838; I have not seen it.

Sull'onda cheta e bruna

Barcarola

Poet unknown

Gaetano Donizetti

Sul - l'on - da che - ta e bru - na,

pria che sor - ga la lu - - - - - - na,

na, ve - lo - ce, o gon - do - liɛr, dɛh, sol - ca il

Ⓐ Sing the grace notes quickly and before the beat.

Literal translation: Over the silent, dark water, just before moonrise, set out quickly, gondolier.

(b) Sing the double grace notes quickly and on the beat, as indicated by the accent mark.

But be careful that your boat caresses the sea lightly. Leonora, who is singing anxiously all the while, should be able to hear only the beating heart of her faithful lover and your quiet rowing.

Ti sento, sospiri

(I hear you sighing)

ti   sɛnto   sospiːri
1 Ti   sento,   sospiri,
You I-hear, you-sigh,

ti   laɲːɲi   damoːre
2 Ti   lagni   d'amore:
you complain about-love,

ma ssɔfːfri   mio kɔːre
3 Ma soffri,   mio core,
but you-suffer, my   heart,

maimpara   ttatʃer
4 Ma impara a   tacer;
but learn   to be-silent,

ke   tʃɛnto   martiːri
5 Che   cento   martiri
because hundred torments

kompɛnsaun   pjatʃer
6 Compensa un   piacer.
recompenses one pleasure.

Poetic idea: "You are suffering, my heart, but you will be re-paid with happiness."

Donizetti's use of a text by Metastasio (1698–1782) indicates that this song may be a very early composition. The complete poetic works of Metastasio could be found on the bookshelves of every cultured Italian, and so they were available to a young composer who did not yet have friends to write texts for him. Metastasio's opera librettos were regarded as old-fashioned in Donizetti's time, but they were still admired as models of poetic elegance. Vaccai used texts from Metastasio in his vocal exercises, and Rossini had a favorite Metastasian text, *"Mi lagnerò tacendo,"* which he set to music dozens of times.

"Ti sento, sospiri" comes not from an opera but from a group of brief, single-stanza poems that Metastasio wrote and himself set to music in the form of vocal canons.

Line 3: *sospiri* should be understood in the sense of "tolerate, bear, endure," according to Mario Fubini and Ettore Bonora, the editors of Metastasio's *Opere* (Milan: Ricciardi, 1968).

Line 8: *un piacer* is not "a pleasure," but "one pleasure," which is enough to counterbalance a hundred troubles.

Measure 25 contains the instruction *portando la voce.* The syllable *-cer* is slurred from its written note up to the pitch of the next note before the syllable *che* is sung on the new pitch. Vaccai, writing in 1832, said that the singer should move smoothly from one pitch to the other and not drag the voice through the intervening pitches.

Source: Autograph manuscript, Paris, Ms. 4180. Original key: E major. Heading, *"Romanza."*

Weinstock listed this song incorrectly as *"Si tanto sospiri, ti lagni d'amore."* UTET and New Grove adopted this listing without examining the Paris manuscript. UTET suggested, also incorrectly, that this piece is identical with a duet for women's voices that was published in *Donizetti per camera.*

Ti sento, sospiri

Pietro Metastasio

Gaetano Donizetti

Literal translation: I hear you sighing; you are complaining of love. But suffer, my heart, and

ⓐ Perform all grace notes before the beat and quickly.

learn to be silent, because one pleasure will reward you for a hundred sorrows.

Tu mi chiedi s'io t'adoro (You ask me if I love you)

tu   mi kjɛdi sio tadoːro
1 Tu   mi chiedi s'io t'adoro,
You me ask   if-I you-adore,

se ffedele sonoaŋkoːra
2 Se fedele sono ancora,
if faithful I-am still,

seoɲːɲi ʤorno seadoɲːɲoːra
3 Se ogni   giorno, se ad ogn'ora
if every day,   if at every-hour

tu sɛi larbitra   del   kɔr
4 Tu sei l'arbitra   del   cor?
you are   the-arbiter of-the heart?

si mio bɛːne ti   son fiːda
5 Sì, mio bene, ti   son fida,
Yes, my dear, to-you I-am faithful,

a tte pɛnso in oɲːɲistante
6 A te   penso in ogni istante.
of you I-think in every moment

tu sɛi landʒelo la gwiːda
7 Tu sei l'angelo, la guida,
You are the-angel, the guide,

la mia ʤɔja il mio dolor
8 La mia gioia, il mio dolor.
— my joy,   — my sorrow.

Poetic idea: "You ask whether I love you! I do, and you are everything to me."

This text could be sung in many moods, but Donizetti has made it into a cheerful waltz song. Waltzes were the most popular dances of the 1800s, and the musical style was defined and developed in Vienna. As a visitor to Vienna, Donizetti was probably taken to hear the waltz orchestra of Johann Strauss, Sr.

Line 5: *fida,* because the ending is feminine, determines that the song is meant for a woman to sing. If a man sings it, this word must be changed to *fido,* which would weaken the rhyme scheme.

In measure 155 the second fermata affects all of the 32nd notes, slowing all of them down as much as the singer wishes.

"Tu mi chiedi" has the form of a freely unfolding rondo. For memorization it is helpful to note that:
   a) the opening section, measures 9–21, is repeated beginning at measure 44;
   b) a longer segment of the opening section, measures 9–36, is repeated beginning at measure 94;
   c) a brief segment of the opening section, measures 9–12, is repeated beginning at measure 147.

Also, the phrase found in measures 56–58 returns in measures 122–124.

Source: Autograph manuscript, Paris, Ms 4080. Original key: C major.

The manuscript is headed *"Romanza"* and "Donizetti." Apparently, this song has never been published before. According to UTET, it was written in 1840 and dedicated to Zélie de Coussy.

Tu mi chiedi s'io t'adoro

Poet unknown

Gaetano Donizetti

Literal translation: You ask me: do I adore you? Am I still faithful

to you? Every day, every hour, are you still the one who rules my heart? Yes, my dear, I am still faithful to you. I think of you every moment.

You are my angel, my guide, my joy, my sorrow.

de - le so - no an - co - ra,_____ se o - gni
gior - no, se ad o - gn'o - ra tu sei
l'ar - bi - tra_____ del cor?
Ah, mio bε - ne,

(a) Sing "-lor" on the repetition, to finish the word "dolor."
Editor's suggestion: Perform measures 125–140 at a quicker tempo and repeat them at an even quicker tempo.

(b) Editor's suggestion: Connect the first two notes of measure 147 with a portamento and do not breathe until measure 149.

Viva il matrimonio

(Long live marriage)

se tu dʒiːri tutːtɔil mondo
1 Se tu giri tutto il mondo,
If you tour all the world,

kwantoɛ luŋgo largo e ttondo
2 Quanto è lungo, largo e tondo,
however it-is long, wide and round,

sentiɾai del matrimɔːnjo
3 Sentirai del matrimonio
you-will-hear of matrimony

milːleiŋkɔːmodi narːɾar
4 Mille incomodi narrar:
thousand discomforts be-told;

ti diran ke dei malanːni
5 Ti diran che dei malanni,
you they-will-say that with misfortunes,

kwando lwɔːmoɛ mariaːto
6 Quando l'uomo è maritato,
when a-man is married

il vazɛlːlo skoperkjaːto
7 Il vasello scoperchiato
the vessel unlidded

su lui dɛːvesi versar
8 Su lui devesi versar.
on him has-to pour.

somiʎːʎarloauna galɛːra
9 Somigliarlo a una galera,
To-compare-it to a prison,

aun kapɛstro sentiɾai
10 A un capestro, sentirai,
to a noose, you-will-hear,

il moɾir fia mɛːʎːʎoasːsai
11 Il morir fia meglio assai,
the dying would-be better very-much,

ti diɾan delːlo spozar
12 Ti diran, dello sposar.
to-you they-will-say about marrying.

un dʒornoun wɔm di mɛːrito
13 Un giorno un uom di merito,
One day a man of merit

da ttutːtiasːsai stimaːto
14 Da tutti assai stimato,
by all very-much respected,

parlandoaun fidantsaːto
15 Parlando a un fidanzato,
speaking to an engaged-man,

ditʃea kon gravita
16 Dicea con gravità:
said with gravity:

la dɔnːna ɛ danːno e kwindi
17 "La donna è danno, e quindi
"The woman is damage, and so

seal danːno lwɔm sakːkɔpːpja
18 Se al danno l'uom s'accoppia,
if to-the damage the-man himself-pairs-up,

i maːli swɔi radːdɔpːpja
19 I mali suoi raddoppia,
the harms his he-doubles,

ripɔːzo pju non a
20 Riposo più non ha.
rest more not he-has.

pɔi kwandoi fiʎːʎi zbutːtʃano
21 Poi quando i figli sbucciano
Then when the sons emerge

komintʃaunaltra ʃɛːna
22 Comincia un'altra scena,
begins a-different scene;

alːlor la sua katɛːna
23 Allor la sua catena
then the his chain

pjuorːriːbile si fa
24 Più orribile si fa:
more horrible itself makes.

pitːtʃiniːni kol gwa gwa
25 Piccinini col guà, guà;
Little-ones with 'wah wah,'

un pɔadulti kol papa
26 Un po' adulti col papà.
a bit older with 'papa!'

grandi pɔi kon tʃɛntoe tʃɛnto
27 Grandi poi, con cento e cento
Big-ones then with hundred and hundred

kapritʃetːtie stramberiːe
28 Capricetti e stramberie,
little-caprices and eccentricities.

kwal moliːnoin prɛːdal vɛnto
29 Qual molino in preda al vento
That mill in prey to-the wind

la tua tɛsta fan dʒirar
30 La tua testa fan girar."
— your head make spin."

duŋkwe duŋkwe il matrimɔːnjo
31 Dunque, dunque il matrimonio
Then, then the marriage

sol di gwai ɛa nɔi fekondo
32 Sol di guai è a noi fecondo?
only of troubles is to us productive?

nɔ ssiɲ:ɲor pof:far del mondo
33 "No, signor, poffar del mondo,
"No, sir, marvel at-the earth!

kwestaɛ gran bestjalita
34 Questa è gran bestialità.
This is great wrong-thinking.

ma ppuːreil gwa gwa
35 Ma pure il guà, guà,
But just the wah wah,

ma puːreil papa
36 Ma pure il papà.
but just the 'papa!'

se presjɛːdeal matrimɔːnjo
37 Se presiede al matrimonio
If presides in-the marriage

veːro af:fɛt:toe simpatia
38 Vero affetto e simpatia,
true affection and sympathy,

non vɛ ssta:toin feːde mia
39 Non v'è stato, in fede mia,
not there-is state, in faith mine,

ke ppju ljɛːti vi fa star
40 Che più lieti vi fa star.
that more happy you make be

una doltʃe paroliːna
41 Una dolce parolina,
A sweet dear-word,

del:la spɔːzauna moiːna
42 Della sposa una moina,
from-the wife an endearment,

ti faran:no dal:la tɛsta
43 Ti faranno dalla testa
for-you will-make from-the head

mil:le kaŋkeri zgombrar
44 Mille cancheri sgombrar.
thousand tormenting-ideas empty-out.

e dei kaːri bambolet:ti
45 E dei cari bamboletti,
And of-the dear little-babies

le karet:tsed i batʃet:ti
46 Le carezze ed i bacetti
the caresses and the dear-kisses

aŋkei di pju tristiɛ nneːri
47 Anche i dì più tristi e neri
even the days more sad and black

in sereːni fan kandʒar
48 In sereni fan cangiar.
into bright-ones make change.

vjeːni kwa bambolet:to
49 Vieni quà, bamboletto.
Come here, dear-baby.

vjeːni kwa fanʧulet:to tjɛn kwa
50 Vieni quà, fanciuletto. Tien qua...
Come here, dear-boy. Stay here...

vedeːte kwantɛ kaːro vedeːtelo
51 Vedete quant'è caro; vedetelo;
Look how-he-is dear; look-at-him.

kwalke vɔlta ɛ ostinatɛl:lo
52 qualche volta è ostinatello,
Some time he-is a-little-stubborn.

kat:tivut:ʃo ma ppɔi al:loːra
53 cattivuccio, ma poi allora...
a-little-naughty, but then still...

dʒen:narjɛl:lo paskarjɛl:lo
54 Gennariello, Pascariello,
Dear-Gennaro, dear-Pasquale,

margeriːtae mmad:daleːna
55 Margherita e Maddalena,
Margaret and Magdalene

raf:faeːle nan:narɛl:la
56 Raffaele e Nannarella...
Raphael and dear-Nancy...

si duŋkwe viːvail matrimɔːnjo
57 Sì, dunque viva il matrimonio."
Yes, then long-live marriage.

Poetic idea: "However many jokes and complaints you may hear about marriage, a marriage filled with love and children is the happiest life you can have."

The title page of this song calls it a *Cavatina buffa,* a comic aria. It is so long that it resembles the solo cantatas of the Baroque era, with their recitatives and arias in contrasting tempos. The word *cavatina* more normally describes a slow operatic aria that leads into another aria in a faster tempo, called a *cabaletta.* Many solo scenes in Italian operas are designed this way.

The published edition states that this was composed for the marriage of Baron Luigi Compagno to Maria de' Marchesi del Carretto.

This aria uses the full range of comic devices that Rossini and Donizetti developed in their popular operas, including rapid patter, spoken words, nonsense syllables (imitating babies, beginning in measure 55), and falsetto singing (beginning in measure 104).

Although Donizetti's comic genius smiles brightly in this aria, he himself had little of the marital bliss that is depicted. He and his wife Virginia were deeply in love, but they lost all three of their children in infancy and Virginia died in 1837 at the age of 28.

Source: Copy in Milan (Milan: Giovanni Ricordi, no date). Original key: C major. Voice part in bass clef. New Grove gives a publication date of 1843.

Viva il matrimonio

Leopoldo Tarentini

Gaetano Donizetti

Literal translation: If you travel all the great world around, you will hear tell about the thousand faults of marriage. They will tell you that

co - mo-di___ nar - rar: ti di-ran___ che dei___ ma-

lan - ni, quan-do l'uɔ - mo ɛ̀ ma - ri - ta - to, il va-

sɛl - lo sco - per-chia - to su lui de - ve-si___ ver-

sar. So-mi-gliar-lo a u - na ga - lɛ - ra, a un ca-pɛ-stro, sen-ti - ra - i, se tu gi-ri tut-to il

ⓐ Perform the grace note quickly and ahead of the beat.

when a man marries, a potful of misfortunes will pour out upon him. You will hear marriage compared to a galley or to a
noose, and that

death would be much better than marrying. One day a meritorious man,

admired by all, speaking to an engaged friend, said in seriousness: "A woman is harm itself, and so, if a man joins up with harm,

his troubles are doubled; he has no more rest. And when the children come, another scene begins; then his chains are worse
yet. Little ones going 'wah-wah,'

guà, guà, guà, guà, guà; un po' a-dul - ti col pa - pà, pa-pà, pa-pà. Gran-di

po - i, con cɛn-to e cɛn-to ca-pri-cet-ti ɛ stram-be - ri - e, ca-pri-cet-ti ɛ stram-be -

ri - e, qual mo - li-no in prɛ-da al vɛn-to

la tua tɛ - sta fan gi - rar, fan gi - rar, fan gi - rar." Dunque,

bigger ones crying 'papa!' Bigger ones yet with hundreds of tricks and oddities, so your head spins like a windmill." Then

does marriage give us nothing but trouble? "No, sir, not on your life! That's a complete misunderstanding. That's just the 'wah-wah' and the 'papa!' If

true affection and sympathy prevail in marriage, there is no condition, by my faith, that can make you happier. A sweet little word, an endearment from your wife, will put a thousand worries out of your mind.

And the kisses and caresses of the dear little babies can change even your saddest, darkest days into bright ones. Come here, dear baby, come here, dear

boy. Just look, how dear he is; look at him. Sometimes he's a little stubborn, a little naughty, but then…

Gennaro, Pasquale, Margaret and Madeleine, Raphael and Nancy…

riɛl - lo, Mar - ghe - ri - ta e Mad - da - le - na, Raf - fa - e - le e Nan - na - rɛl - la... An - co i dì più tri - sti e

ne - ri in___ se - re - ni fan___ can - giar, in se - re - ni fan can -

giar, in se - re - ni fan can - giar. Sì, dun - que vi - va il ma - tri -

mɔ - - nio.

Yes, then long live marriage!"

Key to the International Phonetic Alphabet (IPA)

Example Words in English	IPA Symbol	Example Words in Italian	Example Words in French
VOWELS			
see [si]	[i]	*si* [si]	*fine* [fin]
chaotic [keɒtɪk]	[e]	*sera* [seːra]	*café* [ka fe]
set [sɛt]	[ɛ]	*bene* [bɛːne]	*mais* [mɛ]
aisle [aɪl]	[a]	*la* [la]	*la* [la]
far [fɑr]	[ɑ]	—	*pas* [pɑ]
ought [ɔt]	[ɔ]	*poco* [pɔːko]	*fort* [fɔr]
obey [obeɪ]	[o]	*solo* [soːlo]	*rose* [roz]
too [tu]	[u]	*tu* [tu]	*tout* [tu]
opera [ɒprə]	[ə]	—	*le* [lə]

The vowels in these words occur only in French, not in English or Italian: *lune* [lyn]; *feu* [fø]; *jeune* [ʒœn]; *an* [ɑ̃]; *fin* [fɛ̃]; *on* [õ]; and *un* [œ̃].

The vowels in these words occur only in English, not in Italian or French: sing [ɪ]; sang [sæŋ]; long [lɒŋ]; good [gʊd]; sung [sʌŋ]; and sir [sɝ].

SEMI-VOWELS (Glides)			
yes [jɛs]	[j]	*più* [pju]	*yeux* [jø]
we [wi]	[w]	*guai* [gwai]	*oui* [wi]
(only in French)	[ɥ]	—	*nuit* [nɥi]

CONSONANTS			
angry [æŋgrɪ]	[ŋ]	*anche* [aŋke]	—
shoe [ʃu]	[ʃ]	*uscio* [uʃːʃo]	*chose* [ʃoz]
measure [mɛɪʒə]	[ʒ]	—	*jamais* [ʒa mɛ]
sets [sɛts]	[ts]	*senza* [sɛntsa]	—
weds [wɛdz]	[dz]	*mezzo* [mɛdːdzo]	—
chow [tʃaʊ]	[tʃ]	*ciao* [tʃao]	—
gem [dʒɛm]	[dʒ]	*già* [dʒa]	—
—	[ɲ]	*ogni* [oɲːɲi]	*agneau* [a ɲo]
(only in Italian)	[ʎ]	*agli* [aʎːʎi]	—

CONSONANTS (continued)

These alphabet letters are used as IPA symbols in all three languages (spellings may vary):
[m, f, v, s, z, b, g].

These consonants are similar in all three languages, with significant differences of articulation:
[d, n, t, l], alveolar in English, dentalized in Italian and French;
[p, t, k], aspirated in English, unaspirated in Italian and French.

The English *r* [ɹ] must be avoided in Italian and French. The uvular *r* [ʀ], used in conversational French, must be avoided in singing. The *r* that is used in Italian and in sung French is produced forward in the mouth; it is either flipped [ɾ] or rolled [r] with the front of the tongue.

These consonant sounds occur only in English:
he [hi]; whip [hwɪp]; thin [θɪn]; this [ðɪs].

The Sounds of Donizetti's Languages

In order to approach each foreign language in the best way, it is useful to compare each with the others and with English. This approach identifies the leading characteristics of each.

Legato, or smooth connection of sounds within a breath/phrase: In English the legato line is often broken for various reasons. Italian is highly legato, except for silences caused by unvoiced doubled consonants. French is almost perfectly legato.

Syllabic stress: English has both weak and strong syllables, with several levels of relative strength. Italian also has weak and strong syllables, but none as weak as an English schwa [ə]. In French all syllables have equal strength except for schwas, which are sometimes omitted completely.

Vowel length: In English the so-called long and short vowels differ in quality, but not necessarily in duration. Italian has long vowels (before single consonants) and short ones (before double consonants) in stressed syllables. In French all vowels have equal length, except that at the end of a breath/phrase the last vowel (except for a schwa) is lengthened.

Consonant strength: English consonants are strong and expressive. Italian consonants are gentle, except for double consonants, which are strongly articulated. French has precise but gentle articulation. English plosive consonants [p, t, k] are spoken with aspiration (a puff of air that reinforces the consonant), but French and Italian plosives are not.

Phonetic transcriptions can only serve as guides for pronunciation, not as final authorities. There are many slight differences between languages that are too subtle to be shown in the IPA. One learns these differences by listening carefully to artistic singers who are performing in their native languages.

Many singers employ vowel modification as part of their personal vocal technique. This book intentionally avoids recommending vowel modifications, which should remain personal choices.

Beyond the basic principle that one symbol should stand for one sound, authorities have developed various styles of transcription that vary in minor ways.

In all of the Italian songs in this book, two kinds of phonetic helps appear.

1) Underlining indicates the sustained vowel of each diphthong because the correct pronunciation may not be clear to a person who is singing at sight.

2) Two IPA symbols, [ɛ] and [ɔ], indicate the open sounds of *e* and *o* in order to save the student from the necessity of writing them in. Italian language textbooks printed in the United States began this practice more than 60 years ago, and it has been found useful in forming habits of correct pronunciation. Of course, native Italians do not need such symbols and do not use them in normal printing.

In conventional IPA transcriptions a stressed syllable is marked with a vertical line, thus [aˈmoːre]. This book employs an innovation made by Dr. Berton Coffin, showing a stressed syllable by underlining, thus [amoːre]. This assists the singer in emphasizing vowels over consonants. Because underlining is also used to show the sustained vowel of a diphthong, there can be more than one underlined vowel in a combination of words, such as *ogni amore* [oɲːɲiamoːre].

Transcriptions of Italian texts in this book take account of two subtleties that have been neglected in earlier published transcriptions.

1) A stressed vowel followed by a single consonant should be lengthened, as in caro [kaːro].

2) Certain combinations of words result in a consonant being doubled in idiomatic pronunciation. For instance, the question *"Chi sa?"* (who knows?) is pronounced [ki ssa], and sometimes it is even written *"Chissà?"*

Transcriptions of French texts follow the example of Dr. Pierre Delattre by showing each syllable individually, not grouped into words. This practice graphically reminds the singer to prolong all vowels and to treat all syllables with relative equality.

Recommended authorities on pronunciation:

Coffin, Delattre, Errolle and Singer, *Phonetic Readings of Songs and Arias.* (Metuchen, NJ: Scarecrow Press, 1982.)
Warnant, *Dictionnaire de la prononciation française.* (Paris: Duculot, 1987.)
Zingarelli, *Vocabolario della lingua italiana,* 11th edition. (Bologna: Zanichelli, 1990.)